George C. Marshall,
Man Behind the Plan

Statesman and Retirement Years, 1945-1959

"In war, he was as wise in understanding and counsel as he was res-olute in action. In peace, he was the architect who planned the restoration of our battered European economy and, at the same time, laboured tirelessly to establish a system of Western defense. He has always fought victoriously against defeatism, discouragement, and disillusion. Succeeding generations must not be allowed to forget his achievements, and his example."

Sir Winston Churchill

ISBN 0966158237

Published by Blue Valley Books
            103 Johnstone Street
            Lexington VA 24450

Other books by Mary Sutton Skutt
Growing Up, By George! George C. Marshall's early years, 1880-1901.
Published 1997.
George C. Marshall, *Reporting for Duty* in the U.S. Army, 1902-1945.
Published 2001.

Photographs and illustrations courtesy of the George C. Marshall
Research Library Archives and Virginia Military Institute Archives,
Lexington, Virginia

Cover design by Jeanne Pedersen, Director of Graphic Designs,
George C. Marshall Foundation, Lexington, Virginia

This book is dedicated to my twelve grandchildren, especially two of
them, Joseph Thomas LaFalce and Mary Kathryn Puglisi because Joe
and Mary are eleven years old this year. I was eleven when George C.
Marshall gave what we now call "the Harvard Speech," announcing
ideas for a European recovery plan. I want young people, including
my grandchildren, to learn about George C. Marshall. General
Marshall's life proves that a normal, ordinary boy (or girl) can grow
into a dedicated public servant who lives with faith and integrity and
makes important contributions to national and world history.

Mary Sutton Skutt
November 2004

Printed by the News-Gazette Print Shop
109 South Jefferson Street
Lexington VA 24450

* * * * *

George C. Marshall, Man Behind the Plan
statesman and retirement years, 1945-1959

* * * * *

Contents

1885

1901

1918

1891

1941

Introducing *George C. Marshall, Man Behind the Plan*

George C. Marshall is worthy of study and emulation, especially by today's students. In addition to his historic record of service to the nation in the 20th century, he is the perfect timeless example of a leader: honorable, determined, disciplined and straight talking. He possessed an uncommon blend of genuine idealism and practical realism.

Mary Skutt has written two previous volumes, specifically for young people, about Marshall and has now completed her third book, <u>George C. Marshall, Man Behind the Plan.</u> The first two books, <u>Growing Up, By George!</u> and <u>George C. Marshall, Reporting for Duty,</u> fit into the elementary and middle school years, but the third book is designed for older students and addresses his contributions as a patriot and a statesman, featuring his work with the Marshall Plan. Skutt not only tells of Marshall as a bigger-than-life historical figure, but also of Marshall the human, using personal and family related aspects of his life in the years after World War II.

<u>George C. Marshall, Man Behind the Plan</u> is an excellent work that helps to define this great, but under-recognized man. I recommend this book for contemplative, but enjoyable, reading by teenagers or, for that matter, anyone unfamiliar with George C. Marshall, a true American hero.

Harry H. Warner
President of the George C. Marshall Foundation
October 1, 2004

Timeline of George C. Marshall's Life

December 31, 1880	Born in Uniontown, Pennsylvania
September 11, 1897	June 1901 Cadet, Virginia Military Institute
February 2, 1902	U.S. Army commission - second lieutenant of Infantry
February 11, 1902	Married Elizabeth Carter Coles in Lexington, Virginia
September 15, 1927	Death of Elizabeth C. (Lily) Marshall
October 15, 1930	Married Katherine Tupper Brown, in Washington, DC
September 1, 1939	Sworn in as Chief of Staff, U.S. Army
December 16, 1944	Appointed General of the Army (temporary) with five stars
November 18, 1945	Retired as Chief of Staff, U.S.Army
November 27, 1945	January 20, 1947 – Appointed Special Envoy to China
April 11, 1946	Became General of the Army (permanent)
January 21, 1947 - January 20, 1949	United States Secretary of State
February 28, 1947	Retired from active military service, but not from the Army.
June 5, 1947	Speech given at Harvard University
January 26, 1949 - October 16, 1959	American Battle Monuments chairman
October 1, 1949 - November 30, 1950	President of the American Red Cross
September 12, 1950 - September 12, 1951	United States Secretary of Defense
June 1953	Chairman, U.S. Delegation to Coronation of Queen Elizabeth II
December 10, 1953	Awarded Nobel Prize for Peace
October 16, 1959	Died in Walter Reed Army Hospital
October 19, 1959	Buried in Arlington National Cemetery

Who in the World *Was* George C. Marshall?

George C. Marshall, Man Behind the Plan (statesman and retirement years, 1945-1959) is the last in a trio of books for young people of upper elementary, middle school, and high school ages, covering the life of George C. Marshall (1880 - 1959). The first two books, *Growing Up, By George!* (1998) and *George C. Marshall, Reporting for Duty* (2001), give the facts, figures, and happenings of the first sixty-four years of General Marshall's life; *Man Behind the Plan* covers the last fifteen years.

George Catlett Marshall, Jr. was born on the last day, December 31, of the year 1880. He was the youngest child of George C. Marshall and Laura Bradford Marshall and had one brother, Stuart, and one sister, Marie. They lived in a two-story brick house on West Main Street in Uniontown, Pennsylvania, where his father was a businessman in the coal industry.

George Marshall, Jr. was a normal, inquisitive, and active boy, into and out of mischief, who loved outdoor adventure. He had problems with school, struggling with reading, spelling, and arithmetic, and he did not like to study. His handwriting was never pretty! He listened well, however, and liked history and sports. After 16 years in Uniontown, he went to the Virginia Military Institute in Lexington, Virginia in September of 1897, where he spent the next four years, returning home only during school vacations. He graduated in June of 1901.

After VMI, where he was the top military student in his class each year, he earned a commission in the U.S. Army and was married in February, 1902. He then began his long climb through the army ranks from second lieutenant to general. His career took him to army posts in at least seven different states and across the oceans to the Philippine Islands, France, England, and China.

His progress toward being general was slow and sometimes frustrating for him, taking thirty-four years, but it was the main goal of his life. His talents for organizing, planning, and strategy made him so valuable as a staff officer that his superiors never assigned him to lead troops into battle, for fear of losing him. He was appointed by President Franklin D. Roosevelt to be Chief of Staff of the U.S. Army, the highest army position of all, and was sworn in on September 1, 1939, the same day that World War II began in Europe.

The United States Army had less than 200,000 men in 1939, but Chief of Staff Marshall directed the build-up, training, and deployment of 8,000,000 men and women during World War II. It was Marshall who selected the officer corps, who picked the generals, and who played a leading role in planning military development and operations around the world.

As written in a George C. Marshall Foundation web site article, which you might find at www.marshallfoundation.org: "Few Americans in the twentieth century have left a greater legacy to world peace than George C. Marshall."

British Prime Minister Winston Churchill called General Marshall "the true organizer of victory." General George C. Marshall was known for his honesty, fairness, patriotism, unselfishness, and leadership. He retired as Chief of Staff in 1945, but he did not retire from active service to his country, and that point in his life is where this story begins.

*　*　*　*　*

Man Behind the Plan

Chapter 1

Putting a Plan into Play

September 1945

General of the Army George C. Marshall was a man with a plan. In September of 1945, World War II had ended and he was ready for his army career to be over, too. It was time to pass his job along to another general. After all, he had served his country for forty-three and a half years, beginning as a second lieutenant in 1902 and ending as the army's highest-ranking officer, chief of staff (1939-1945). Some people are afraid to stop working, but he was not; George C. Marshall had plenty of plans ready to try, such as traveling, fishing and hunting. His sixty-fifth birthday was only three months away, so surely the time for retirement had arrived. He liked the sound of that word, retirement, and planned to use it often.

Katherine Marshall thought retirement was a wonderful idea for her husband. He deserved a much-needed rest from duty and heavy responsibilities. The three years and nine months of world-wide war (December 1941—August 1945) had taken their toll on General Marshall's health and personality. Katherine Marshall wrote about those changes in her book, *Together, Annals of an Army Wife,* "Mentally and physically he was a very weary man." Two pictures of the General, which she had named "Before" and "After," stood on the bureau in her bedroom. She said they clearly showed the changes that had taken place in his appearance and attitude.

About the first picture, taken in 1938, before General Marshall left Vancouver Barracks in Washington State to work in the War Plans Division in Washington DC, Katherine wrote, "In this photograph, his arms are folded; there is a calm expression in his eyes and few lines in his face. His hair is auburn, his figure slight. There is an inscrutable smile on his face. It is my favorite picture, for it shows a man at peace with himself and with his world."

2

June 1938

April 1945

The second picture, she said, "shows a deeply lined face, set jaw, eyes of steel, grey hair, and an expression such as you could hardly believe possible for the face in the first picture. There is only cold calculated determination and indomitable will in that face. There is no peace."

George C. Marshall would never lose interest in serving his country, but in the summer of 1945, he needed a change and some rest. Because Marshall's job was a presidential appointment, he needed the president's consent to retire, so he wrote a letter to President Harry S. Truman asking for retirement. By October, both he and Katherine were slightly impatient for an answer.

In the evenings, when he came home to Quarters One at Fort Myer, from his Pentagon office, she would ask, "Did you see the President today?" and she received about the same answer night after night, "No, he is over-burdened with problems on the home front. I do not wish to push the issue." President Truman, his Cabinet, and the Congress had plenty to keep them busy following the war. Still, the Marshalls kept hoping that good news for them would soon come from the President.

Also in late August, Secretary of War Henry L. Stimson announced he would retire. Like Marshall, he had served his country long and well. The two had worked together throughout WWII and had great respect for each other. Stimson was seventy-eight years old and felt the need of a rest even more than Marshall. In one of Stimson's last acts as war secretary, he suggested to President Truman that a specific Congressional Medal be made for General Marshall as an expression of the nation's appreciation for his hard work as chief of staff. That medal is on display in the George C. Marshall Museum in Lexington, Virginia.

Stimson wrote to Truman, "General Marshall's leadership takes its authority directly from his great strength of character. I have never known a man who seemed so surely to breathe the democratic American spirit. . . His trust in his commanders is almost legendary. . . He likewise is the most generous of men, keeping himself in the background so that his subordinates may receive all credit for duties well done. His devotion to the nation he serves is a vital quality, which infuses everything he does. The destiny of America at the most critical time of its national existence has been in the hands of a great and good citizen. Let no man forget it."

Chief of Staff Marshall talks with Secretary of War Stimson.

President Truman respected and depended on General Marshall, and he agreed that Marshall could retire from active duty, but not from the Army. Marshall had done an excellent job as chief of staff, and with his recommendation, the President appointed General Dwight D. Eisenhower, the famous leader of the June 6, 1944 D-Day Invasion, to take his place. It must have been a relief to transfer the responsibility of the entire U.S. Army into younger and trusted hands. Marshall had reached his lifetime goal in serving as chief of staff, but six years of stress and worry had been enough.

The Marshalls wanted and deserved to have some relaxing years of traveling or just staying home doing nothing special. They owned two houses — one named Dodona Manor in Leesburg, Virginia, and one called Liscombe Lodge in Pinehurst, North Carolina. They planned to live in their Leesburg house during the warm weather months and in their Pinehurst cottage during the winter. They had bought the Pinehurst place, barely a year earlier, and they planned to go there as soon as they could. General Marshall hoped to do some autumn quail hunting and watch some golf matches in Pinehurst, travel to the Gulf of Mexico for a bit of fishing in January, take a few trips in his new car, and be back in Virginia in time to work in his garden at Leesburg in the spring-time.

Katherine wrote, "Once more we worked over maps in the evenings," but unlike the maps of Europe and Asia they had stud-ied during the war days, "They were maps of lovely spots in which to rest and relax, maps of automobile routes by which we could enjoy our freedom most. It was great fun planning all this. True, our hair was grey, but there was nothing grey in those plans. The fact is it was to be a long-delayed honeymoon, for we had never had one. We had stepped from the altar into Army activities and had been following Army dictates and routine for fifteen years."

Katherine said in her book, "I cannot tell you how much joy President Truman's decision brought to our home. A great load seemed to roll off my husband's shoulders. At breakfast he was carefree, the heavy lines between his eyes began to disappear, and he laughed once more."

* * * * *

Home of the Army's Chief of Staff -- Quarters I at Fort Myer, Virginia

Man Behind the Plan

Chapter 2

Changing Places

September – November 1945

Retirement became a reality, and they needed to leave their assigned chief of staff's house at Fort Myer, where they had lived for the past six years. They began the move from Quarters One in October, but moving the collected possessions of a forty-three year army career was not an easy task. There were closets full of army clothes, from fatigues to formal uniforms, that he had used in the northern arctic, the tropics, and everywhere in between.

Other closets were filled with souvenirs sent from various and odd sources. There was a large collection, including a piece of marble off of the desk of Adolph Hitler, a stuffed owl, a gold miniature boxing glove labeled "To the Champ", and an antique bronze Chinese sword from the Chin Dynasty, B.C. 255-207—-a valuable museum piece. It is not clear what happened to the stuffed owl, but the Chinese sword, a gift from Dr. T.V. Soong, a brother of Madame Chiang Kai Shek, is in the George C. Marshall Museum in Lexington, Virginia. Katherine counted twenty-six oil paintings of General Marshall, as well as a number of plaques and drawings, some good and some awful. Among the clutter were many flags, captured machine guns, rifles, swords, and even a canteen, with water still in it, from the Bataan Death March in the Philippine Islands. Several closets held boxes full of reports, papers, letters, or books. Moving and sorting was an awesome and necessary chore that only Katherine could do for him.

The General went to the Pentagon early in the mornings to take care of work and pack his office things, while Katherine packed boxes at Quarters One. She supervised the loading and the unloading of trucks, and the moving of their belongings from one place to the other. She followed the trucks to their house, Dodona Manor, in her car and George went to Leesburg in the afternoon in his staff car. While cleaning out Quarters One, the Marshalls took an apartment at the Ft. Myer Officer's Club. There, they awaited the arrival of General and Mrs. Dwight Eisenhower while Dodona Manor awaited them.

One might think there was nothing left for Marshall to do but to hand over the keys to his Pentagon office, but he had never known a time when there was nothing left to do. The war was over, his job was finished, the nation was at peace again, but keeping the peace was frequently on George C. Marshall's mind.

In the fall of 1945, he was still trying to solve a special problem related to peace, one he had been working on and had believed in for years, at least since World War I — Universal Military Training. During his chief of staff years, 1939-1945, Marshall wrote three biennial reports for the Army, explaining when, where, and what had happened. In September 1945, in his third *Biennial Report to the Secretary of War*, he wrote about UMT.

He thought a citizen-soldier army, even in a time of peace, was a good defense for the nation to have. A full-time active army was not necessary, but there should be active reserve forces for all service branches. Marshall thought the purpose of UMT was to avoid war, not to provoke it; "the only way to be sure of winning a third world war is to prevent it," he once said. General Marshall knew that peace would not be easy to keep.

In that third biennial report, Marshall also wrote in favor of the United Nations as an additional force for keeping the peace with international armed forces. He was convinced that the United States had acquired worldwide responsibilities for repairing the damages of war, but the United Nations forces would add strength and support. These ideas, of United Nations troops and the buildup of UMT, were not widely accepted by Congress or the American people at that time. According to Forrest C. Pogue, Marshall's official biographer, in *Statesman*, Marshall would be "selling them" all across the country to the public and to Congress a few years later. In the meantime, he would leave details in the hands of his capable replacement.

General Dwight D. Eisenhower officially replaced George C. Marshall as chief of staff on November 20, 1945. Almost a week later, on November 26, a special retirement ceremony was held for General Marshall in the courtyard of the Pentagon.

Pogue wrote, "The Army band played *Hail to the Chief*, the *Star Spangled Banner*, and the *Spirit of V.M.I.* because Marshall graduated from Virginia Military Institute in 1901." After the music, Marshall made a few brief remarks, but not a formal speech.

He thanked President Truman for ending the war. Then he spoke to those who had served in the War Department with him. He said, "You were the greatest protective force this nation has ever known." To the regular soldiers and the air corps, including those still serving in distant lands, he said, "But for all of these efforts, yours was by far the greatest. You faced death and swallowed fear, endured the agonies of battle and of hearts torn by loneliness and homesickness and starvation for the normal life you loved. Yet you took it—all there was to take on the battlefronts of the world. And you had the strength and will to give it back, give back much more than your enemies could take . . ."

He then spoke to everyone, words similar to the ones he would say a year and a half later at Harvard University, of what lay ahead in terms of fixing the world for a permanent peace. He said this:

"Today this nation with good faith and sincerity, I am certain, desires to take the lead in the measures necessary to avoid another world catastrophe, such as you have just endured. And the world of suffering people looks to us for such leadership." He said that those in war-torn countries were not thinking about the whole problem, but were mainly concerned with their daily problems. "They have the more immediate and terribly pressing concerns —where the next mouthful of food will come from, where they will find shelter tonight and where they will find warmth from the cold of winter. Along with the great problem of maintaining the peace, we must solve the problem of the pittance of food, clothing, coal, and homes. Neither of these problems can be solved alone. They are directly related, one to the other."

President Harry S. Truman presented General Marshall with an Oak Leaf Cluster that he would add to the Distinguished Service Medal he received in World War I. President Truman later remarked

General George C. Marshall receives another decoration from President Harry S. Truman, November 26, 1945.

that no medal or decoration was "big enough to fit General Marshall." Marshall refused medals during the war because he did not think it appropriate to accept them while Americans were being killed, taken as prisoners, and missing in action.

Then, Truman read a lengthy citation, and the following is part of that tribute. "His standards of character, conduct and efficiency inspired the entire Army, the Nation and the world. To him, as much as to any individual, the United States owes its future. He takes his place at the head of the greatest commanders of history."

In *Together*, Katherine Marshall wrote, "More revealing even than citations, commendations, and decorations are the innumerable letters received by General Marshall from American fathers and mothers and from service men and women." She said that Marshall had filing cases filled with these letters and he had answered all of them.

The next day they left Ft. Myer behind and headed for Dodona Manor. They sent an orderly to see that everything at Leesburg was ready for them. Then, they dismissed their chauffeur and drove out to the house together, alone. It was General Marshall's custom to give a lift to anyone who stuck out his thumb for a ride, but that day he did not pick up any hitchhikers. "On this particular afternoon we needed no outsiders to amuse us on our way down to our home. We were full of our own thoughts and plans," Katherine said.

Today there are housing developments, schools, fast food places, stores, strip malls, and service stations along busy, six-lane Route 7 that leads from Tyson's Corner in McLean and narrows into a 2 lane street passing by Dodona Manor. In 1945, the town was still small and the road was less crowded.

In 1945, Mrs. Marshall wrote, "There is a gas station just before you get to the entrance of our place and as we passed it a juke box was blaring out an old and, to me, familiar tune. It had been popular after the First World War and my children used to play it night and day and dance to it until the cottage floor rocked —

Hallelujah! Hallelujah! I could not remember the words, but I began to hum the refrain of *Hallelujah! Hallelujah!*, as we entered our gate. George looked at me and smiled."

> ## Hallelujah
> *Sing Hallelujah — Hallelujah*
> *And you'll shoo the blues away*
> *When cares pursue ya —- Hallelujah*
> *Gets you through the darkest day.*
> *Satan lies awaitin' and creatin' skies of gray*
> *But Hallelujah —- Hallelujah*
> *Helps to shoo the clouds away*

Hallelujah words: Clifford Grey& Leo Robin, music: Vincent Youmans copyright: 1927 by Warner Brothers Music, Cp April 22, 1983 Herald Square Music Co. New York, NY

They stopped in front of the house, stepped from the car, and stood for a few moments on the porch. The autumn sunshine through the trees and the quiet of the afternoon gave both of them a sense of contentment and rest. Everything seemed to be just right, for they were home, at last.

As they went into the house, Katherine said she was going upstairs to take a short rest before dinner. She was halfway up the stairs when the phone rang, but she did not stop. She knew that George would answer it.

An hour later Katherine came back down to find General Marshall lying on the chaise-lounge listening to the radio. The three o'clock news was coming from the radio, and, as she came into the room, she heard, "President Truman has appointed General of the Army George C. Marshall as his Special Ambassadorial Envoy to China. He will leave immediately."

Katherine said, "I stood rooted to the floor. My husband got up and came over to me. He said, 'That phone call as we came in was from the President. I could not bear to tell you until you had had your rest.'" She was flabbergasted.

* * * * *

Man Behind the Plan

Chapter 3

The Chinese Challenge

December 1945 - January 1956

Katherine had not heard or cared who was calling, and the conversation was certainly short. Without so much as a hello, President Truman had said, "General, I want you to go to China for me," and General Marshall had replied, "Yes, Mr. President."

The nation of China was in trouble. A civil war had started and the situation was serious. The United States had business and strategic interests in China and Truman wanted Marshall to go as his representative and to mediate on behalf of the United States between the Chinese Nationalists and the Chinese Communists. Perhaps Marshall's intervention could help the two enemies reach a satisfactory settlement. President Truman felt that if anyone could resolve the China crisis, Marshall could.

Katherine Marshall was amazed that her husband had agreed so easily to the President's request. She was very disappointed to have their recent retirement plans so quickly dashed to pieces. After all, had the General not said only a few days earlier, at the retirement ceremony, that "the task of making the peace a lasting one" was up to younger people? Perhaps Katherine wondered how long the "mission" would be and when they could resume their own peace plans. She probably wondered why he had to accept the assignment. They were not even a week away from the working world.

Although his retirement had lasted barely a week, George C. Marshall could not refuse. He saw the request from the President as a challenge, one more mission in the service of his country, and to serve his country was the mission of his life. George C. Marshall always put duty and service to his president before his own plans or wishes. He knew the problems in China were enormous, and

**Marshall heads to Senate hearing,
December 1945**

Some China to Mend

that he might fail. George C. Marshall could not shy away from duty; he could not refuse to serve his country, or the President who trusted him. If one does not try, one cannot fail, but he could not turn down the chance to try.

Truman's call came on November 27, and within three weeks, General Marshall was on his way to China. It was not a restful three weeks, at that. In addition to packing for China, George C. Marshall was required to testify in five sessions before a congressional committee. He was questioned by a Senate subcommittee and asked to account for his time during the weeks and days prior to the Japanese attack at Pearl Harbor on December 7, 1941, The committee wanted to know where Marshall was, during the day and night, before the Japanese planes destroyed U.S. ships and planes killing thousands of U.S. service men.

After almost two weeks of questioning, the majority of the congressional committee cleared General Marshall of any neglect of duty with regard to Pearl Harbor. As he left the Senate Caucus Room, the audience stood and applauded. The people listening to his testimony believed in Marshall, even if some senators did not. The whole ordeal left Marshall tired and rather short on packing time. He also needed to prepare mentally for the challenge ahead of him.

He talked at length with President Truman agreeing that he would do the job as he saw fit and that he would keep the President fully advised. He knew that General Chiang Kai-shek was the leader of the Nationalist Party, which the United States supported. On the other side was Mao Tse-tung, the leader of the Chinese Communist Party, whose army was backed by the Soviet Union. Mao's army and political party were also determined to win. Truman expected Marshall to encourage understanding between the two conflicting sides to bring the Chinese Nationalists and the Chinese Communists into a unified government. If that did not happen, eventually, the Soviet Union would likely govern China. Marshall promised to do his best.

China, a country about the size of the United States, and George C. Marshall had an enormous problem. Some U.S. leaders thought that perhaps Chiang's government officials had a good chance of building a democratic, pro-American government. Chiang Kai-shek,

Marshall arrives in China, December 20, 1945.

at least, thought his military leaders and army could win a civil war, especially if their side had U.S. backing. President Truman told Marshall that whatever settlement was reached, the leader in charge of the central government must be Chiang Kai-Skek, if U.S. support was to continue.

General Marshall landed in the city of Shanghai on December 20, 1945, on a cold and snowy day. His first impression of the city, with its evidences of war, was gloomy and depressing. It did not get much better.

The leaders of both sides knew and respected General Marshall, and they agreed to talk with him. For three months, he met with the leaders and the top military officers from both sides. George C. Marshall was diligent; he tried very hard to develop useful talks and understanding between them. By March, they had reached a cease-fire, and he thought they were making progress toward a military agreement. Thinking he might succeed in his assignment, Marshall came back to Washington to seek more U.S. financial support of the Chinese Nationalists.

FIFTEEN CENTS   MARCH 25, 1946

TIME
THE WEEKLY NEWSMAGAZINE

GENERAL MARSHALL
"We must not waste the victory."

VOLUME XLVII   NUMBER 12

Marshall's picture was on the March 25, 1946 cover of *Time*, a national weekly news magazine , and he was referred to as, "the tall man with a weathered, homely face in which there was the visible touch of greatness," and that he was on "the most significant mission undertaken by a U.S. citizen since the end of World War II."

When he returned to China in April, he took Mrs. Marshall with him, as Madame Chiang Kai-shek had requested. The Marshalls hoped his mission would be finished in another few months. They had living quarters in the city of Nanking, in a compound where other members of Marshall's staff lived and where the meeting room, used for their many talks, was located. At times, the meeting room became a recreation room by day and a movie theater at night. The Marshalls settled in for "the duration."

Unhappily, when Marshall returned to China, he was surprised, and not at all pleased, to find the Nationalists and the Communists ready to begin active fighting again. The situation did not look promising, but Marshall did not give up easily. Chiang Kai-shek was not a strong leader, there was corruption in his government ranks, and his military staff was not able to control or lead their forces effectively. He tried talking firmly with Chiang, but made no progress. Sometimes Chiang was unfriendly to Marshall in public and not easy for Marshall to talk with, even with an interpreter.

Regardless of his political conflicts with Chiang Kai-shek, General and Mrs. Marshall were on friendly social terms with him, and especially with his wife, Soong Mei-ling, Madame Chiang Kai-shek. She had been educated in the United States, spoke fluent English, and had interests similar to Katherine Marshall. She and the Marshalls became good friends that spring and stayed friends for many years. Madame Chiang was especially helpful that summer by offering Katherine a place to stay.

Marshall described the weather of late spring and early summer as "hot and swampy even beyond Washington" and he was concerned for Katherine's health. That made visits to the Chiang's summer home a treat. Madame Chiang invited Mrs. Marshall to spend the summer as her guest at their place, on top of a mountain at Kuling, 250 miles from Nanking.

There, Katherine had a cottage of her own, with servants and a small swimming pool, plus shady trees. Sometimes General Marshall went for visits, as did Chiang Kai-shek. Since Madame Chiang spoke English, she was the interpreter between the two men. The atmosphere was socially pleasant, but conversation was not easy.

It was not easy to get to Kuling from Nanking, either. When Marshall went for visits, he took a plane for 2 hours, then a forty-five minute ride by gunboat on the Yangtze River, a thirty-minute car ride, and finally a two hour and fifteen minute ride in a sedan chair carried by six men up steps cut out of the mountainside. Whenever Marshall went, he usually stayed awhile!

Upon his return to Nanking, he went back to work. On May 6, General Marshall wrote to President Truman, "the outlook is not promising," for he did not think the Nationalist forces would escape defeat by the Communists. A few days later in May, General Eisenhower came for a visit with the Marshalls while traveling on an inspection tour of Army bases in the Far East. Eisenhower was a welcome guest and he enjoyed visiting with the Marshalls and General and Madame Chiang Kai-Shek. After lunch, he delivered a private message sent to George C. Marshall from President Truman.

Mrs. Marshall takes a ride up a mountain to Kuling in China.

The U.S. Secretary of State, James Byrnes, was retiring, and Truman wanted Marshall to be the next to fill the position. Marshall was probably expecting this message, because Truman had hinted earlier that he would be asking him, and he had his answer ready. He told Eisenhower to tell Truman "yes" that he would agree to the offer, but that he could not leave China before September. General Eisenhower took Marshall's answer back to Washington, and President Truman was delighted to receive it.

Marshall could not leave until he had tried everything he knew to do to settle the conflict between the Nationalist and Communist Chinese. He stayed on because leaders from both sides of the Chinese argument begged him to stay. Through the summer and into the fall, Marshall continued his efforts to bring the two sides together, but found only disappointment and frustration. Finally, he decided he had done everything he possibly could, even though the conflict continued.

George C. Marshall hated to admit failure, but after a full year, and three hundred meetings, he found no answer to the massive problems of China. He had done his best, but it was time for the Chinese to resolve their problems; he would return to the United States and tackle his. Following an agreement he had made earlier with Truman, he left China on January 8, 1947, the day after the President announced in Washington that George C. Marshall would be the next U.S. Secretary of State.

This time Mrs. Marshall was not taken by surprise when President Truman announced a new appointment for her husband. Their retirement plans, made over a year ago, would be put on hold again. Their Leesburg and Pinehurst life, or any extended travel and leisure, must wait a while longer for them.

* * * * *

Man Behind the Plan

Chapter 4

Wearing a New Hat

January - February 1946

The good part about changing jobs again for George C. Marshall was that, by stopping in Hawaii, he had a short vacation. George C. Marshall was not one for taking vacations; he was always too busy. Upon leaving China, however, George caught up with Katherine, who had left a few weeks earlier, and they spent several days together in Hawaii. The cottage where they stayed was in a grove of palm trees, beside the ocean, and was definitely a welcome change of scene and activity. He was glad for a spell of quiet rest.

From Hawaii, George C. Marshall wrote a letter to his god-daughter, Rose Page Wilson. She says in her book, *General Marshall Remembered*, that he was "taking it easy" —- "loafing on the beach most of the day"—- in the shade of the palm trees in the morning and on the sand in the later afternoon. Those were the days before sunscreen, so George Marshall, with his sandy-colored hair and fair skin, probably did not linger long in the day's bright sunshine, but a shady spot on the beach was welcome.

Also, Rose learned from his letter that Katherine had her Chinese maid traveling with her, so she knew "Colonel Marshall" was enjoying delicious food. He told her they were provided with a Cadillac and a chauffeur for their vacation use. That caused Rose Wilson to laugh, and she wrote, "It was the epitome of luxury to Colonel Marshall! In all his years as an important world figure, I don't think (he) ever got over a kind of child-like surprise and pleasure that he was in a position to enjoy certain creature comforts above the average." Yet, with all the good food and creature comforts, work was never far from the mind of George C. Marshall.

Marshall wrote that his plane was "all ready to go" at a moment's notice if the President should need him in Washington

The Marshalls strolling in Hawaii, January 1947

sooner than planned. General Marshall said that his beach time was "interrupted by 30 messages a day, at the least, some of them quite wordy, with usually one from Sir Winston Churchill."

To Rose Page Wilson, General Marshall was always "Colonel Marshall," because that was his army rank in 1919, when she met him in the elevator of their apartment house. She was about eight years old at the time. At that time, Marshall was working in Washington, DC, as an aide to General of the Armies John J. Pershing, then U.S. Army Chief of Staff. Colonel Marshall and his first wife, Lily, lived in the same apartment building, at 2400 16th Street, as Rose and her family did.

Both of the Marshalls were good friends of hers, and Rose chose him to be her godfather when she was confirmed in the Episcopal Church at age eleven. She and the Colonel remained steadfast friends until he died. Lily died in 1927 and George married Katherine, who was a widow with three children, in 1930. Rose was not as close to the second Mrs. Marshall as she was to the first, but she never lost touch with the Colonel. She was glad to hear from him at any time.

**General Marshall with his goddaughter,
Rose Page Wilson, in Durham, NC, 1950**

All in all, Marshall wrote "a wandering, chatty letter" and Mrs. Wilson "could just visualize him propped up in a beach chair, writing away between intervals of gazing out at the sea or dropping off for a little snooze. As he had all his life, (he) was taking full advantage of his respite from work and worry to build his energies for ordeals that lay ahead." It was a good thing, because he would soon need that energy.

The November 1946 congressional elections created problems for the Democrats because the Republicans won the most seats in both the House of Representatives and in the Senate. President Truman needed someone, regardless of politics, that Congress would trust to take charge of the nation's foreign affairs as Secretary of State. He knew that Congress certainly trusted and respected George C. Marshall during WWII. By December, Washington gossip said that General Marshall was coming back from China and that he was Truman's choice for the job. Sometimes rumors prove true.

After Congress approved the President's choice, the Marshalls left Hawaii and headed for home. They flew to Los Angeles on January 18 and visited briefly with Frank McCarthy, who had been on Marshall's staff during WWII and had gone into the movie producing business after the war. In 1970, McCarthy received an Oscar as producer of the movie *Patton*, and today that Oscar is on display at the Marshall Museum in Lexington, Virginia. From Los Angeles, they flew to Chicago, but the weather turned bad and the plane was delayed, so they rode the train to Washington on January 21 and arrived a day later than planned.

Colonel Marshall S. Carter, one of Marshall's staff, and a number of news reporters greeted them at Union Station in Washington when their train arrived. Carter handed the General a note alerting him that a movement was underway to nominate him for president. The news reporters would likely ask about it, he told Marshall.

The main worry Republicans had about Truman's new Cabinet member was that he might run for President, maybe as a Democrat, even though many knew that Marshall was not a politician. Perhaps they had forgotten he had said, "My father was a Democrat, my mother a Republican, but I am an Episcopalian."

Right then and there, George C. Marshall squelched that idea. To him, it was absurd. He told reporters that his retirement was already being postponed for the second time and "I will never become involved in political matters and therefore I cannot be considered a candidate for any office."

George C. Marshall was sworn in as Secretary of State at the White House on January 21, 1947 by Chief Justice Fred Vinson while President Truman and James F. Byrnes, the former Secretary of State, watched. The happy President smiled widely as he shook Marshall's hand and thanked him for taking on "this burden." Marshall replied, without a smile, that he would do his best. Then, Truman, Byrnes, and Marshall had lunch together and a long, long talk.

Secretary of State Marshall with former Secretary James F. Byrnes and President Truman, January 21, 1947

The job of the Secretary of State is to represent the President and the U.S. government in dealings with the countries of the world. Marshall's job was to obtain all the facts and choices, confer with foreign heads of state, offer advice to the President on problems regarding U.S. policy, and to support the President and Congress in their final decisions. Truman's choice of Marshall was one of his best moves as president. If Marshall had refused to serve, world history might have taken a different turn.

For the most part, the American people were pleased with Marshall's appointment. Henry Stimson wrote to Marshall, "Your appointment as Secretary of State has filled me with a great sense of security so far as our country is concerned. Mr. Truman made a wise, as well as a very shrewd, appointment."

Truman, as well as Congress, appreciated Marshall's sense of duty, integrity, and service to others. He was known for his patriotism and fairness, and for his ability to lead. The testimony of popular government officials, his record as the army chief of staff, and the high regard and respect of all of Congress helped Marshall gain the American people's confidence. Truman said, "He (Marshall) was a man you could count on to be truthful in every way, and when you find somebody like that, you have to hang on to them."

Yet, some people expressed concern because a military career man was given the highest civilian appointment in the government. Usually the Secretary of State was a successful lawyer or businessman and George C. Marshall was neither. Those who worried about his military past causing Marshall to be unfair in his new job felt better when they heard him say, in reference to China, "Though I speak as a soldier, I must also deplore the dominating influence of the military. Their dominance accentuates the weakness of the civil government." With that, the General went to work.

He spent his first days in his new job in the old State, War, and Navy Building at 17th and Pennsylvania Avenue in downtown Washington. In February 1902, two days after his marriage to Elizabeth Carter ("Lily") Coles he had reported, as ordered by the U.S.Army, to the same building. He had been twenty-one years old, a VMI graduate, and his commission as a second lieutenant was less than two weeks old.

Marshall had also worked in that building in 1919-1924 when he was an aide to General John J. Pershing, and then again in 1938 when President Roosevelt called him from Vancouver Barracks to head the War Plans Division of the U.S. Army's General Staff. Working in the same building where he had spent a considerable amount of time was like coming home, but the space was too limited. His home needed remodeling; a larger office building was necessary.

One of his first decisions was to approve the moving of the State Department from 17th and Pennsylvania Avenue into the building at 21st Street and Virginia Avenue. That building had been vacated by the U.S. Army officials when their offices were moved in 1941, into the brand new Pentagon building located across the Potomac River in Virginia.

Another early decision was to reorganize the State Department and make it "his type" of operation. Forrest C. Pogue wrote that George C. Marshall was not one for making "wholesale staff changes when he took over a new position," so he kept the main staff members, added some new ones, and changed a few office procedures.

Two that stayed were Dean G. Acheson, Under Secretary of State, and Will L. Clayton, Under Secretary for Economic Affairs. Next, Marshall summoned Robert A. Lovett, who had worked with him in the development of the Air Forces during WWII, to be an assistant to Clayton. Lovett agreed to accept the job when Marshall told him that he would be the next Under Secretary, replacing Dean Acheson, within a year. To round out the crew, he brought in Colonel Marshall S. Carter as his personal assistant, to be the one in charge of State Department correspondence. These four men proved vitally important to George C. Marshall, as he continued his new career of statesman.

Dean Acheson was Marshall's assistant for six months, and this suited Marshall just fine. He and Acheson were quite different in personality, but they worked well together, respected each other and their individual achievements. In talking to Forrest Pogue about Marshall, Acheson said, "As a commander in charge of the department, he was most unmilitary in regard to his attitude of approach."

Marshall did not want people to try to please *him*, or to do something just because they thought he would like it done. They were to do their very best job, in their own way, and that was that. Marshall was hard-hearted and impatient toward those trying to impress him or those who were self-promoting. He had little patience with those who could not work as a team member; he led by example being always mindful that he himself was part of the team. He was, however, forever patient and understanding with people who were sincerely doing their best and strongly believed in what they were doing.

Although some of his staff remained the same, the way things were done changed quickly. The staff contained several retired army colonels and generals, left over from the James Byrnes days, and Marshall's office routine was left over from his army office days. Pogue quotes from *A Program of Management Reform for the Department of State* (the Marshall Library News Letter, V. 11, No.2, winter '71). "George Marshall was an orderly man, a master of administration and, as a result of his enormous responsibilities during the Second World War, an effective manager of staff.

"Marshall would assign primary responsibility to one office for a given issue, instructing it to consult with all other interested parties, clearly setting out problems and options. He would then hold that office accountable for its recommendations, and come down hard and quickly if the office did its work poorly or failed to consult fully."

No longer did every department head bring his or her projects and ideas straight to the Secretary of State for approval. Dean Acheson learned to screen projects and handle the easy decisions, weed out the trivial, and consolidate the problems before bringing major projects or problems to Marshall's attention. Not every change that Marshall made was a lasting one, but many stayed on after he left office. Marshall and the State Department staff became active and effective players on the Truman diplomatic team.

* * * * *

Man Behind the Plan

Chapter 5

Moscow in March

February – May 1947

A month to the day after Marshall's swearing in, a call came from the British Embassy in Washington to the State Department. The message from Great Britain was that, with so many money problems of its own, Britain must stop supporting the countries of Greece and Turkey. Without enough military and economic support, the two countries would fall to the Soviet Union, and communism, instead of democracy, would be the rule of both. Could the United States possibly help?

The head of the State Department would consider the problem a few days later, but on February 21, 1947, General Marshall was busy receiving an honorary degree from Columbia University, along with several other World War II heroes. Then, on February 22, General and Mrs. Marshall went to Princeton University where he gave his first speech as Secretary of State.

He told the Princeton students and faculty to think about the past, to study history in order to understand the present, and to become involved in the actions of government. Parts of this 1947 speech still apply today.

General Marshall said, "I feel that we are seriously failing in our attitude toward the international problems whose solution will largely determine our future. The public appears generally in the attitude of a spectator. Spectators of life are not those who will retain their liberties nor are they likely to contribute to their country's security. I am therefore greatly concerned that the young men and women of this country, . . .the students in every university, college, and high school in the United States, shall acquire a genuine understanding of lessons of history as they relate to governments

and the characteristics of nations and peoples, and as to the causes
of the wars which have destroyed so much of human life and
progress. . ." He stressed that memorizing the dates of historic
events had little value. "The important thing is to understand the
lessons of these historic events and periods."

Returning to Washington, he began working on the problem of
Greece and Turkey, two side-by-side countries not far from Russia.
Marshall's staff, including Dean Acheson, Charles Bohlen, and
George F. Kennan, had made a quick but detailed study for him.
Once all the facts were gathered, and possible solutions put on
paper, Marshall and Acheson took the problem to President
Truman.

In their meeting with the President, George C. Marshall said, "A
crisis of the utmost importance and urgency has arisen in Greece
and to some extent in Turkey. This crisis has a direct and intimate
relation to the security of the United States. . . .It is not alarmist to
say that we are faced with the first crisis of a series which might
extend Soviet domination to Europe, the Middle East, and Asia. . .
.We are at a point of decision. We cannot enter upon the first steps
of policy without the assurance and determination to carry it
through. To do this requires the support of Congress and certain
legislation. I hope this legislation may be obtained with bipartisan
support and without protracted controversy. Internal division and
delay might gravely imperil the success of the program we are pro-
posing."

Marshall and his staff wrote the speech that the President would
deliver, but left Truman to decide what the exact policies should be,
while Marshall tackled another major assignment, the Moscow
Foreign Ministers Conference.

Marshall went to Moscow to meet with the heads of state from
Great Britain, France, and the Soviet Union. The purpose of the
Foreign Ministers Conference was to discuss the fate of Germany,
the defeated power of WWII, its peace treaty, and the reconstruction
of its devastated economic and political conditions.

The war had been over for a year and a half, yet settlements
remained to be worked out between governments. George C.
Marshall went to Moscow feeling much the way he had felt when
leaving for China. He was not optimistic about achieving quick

Foreign Ministers Conference in Moscow, March 1947
Left to right: Ernest Bevin, George C. Marshall, Vyacheslav Molotov,
and Georges Bidault

agreements and was prepared for lengthy discussions. Yet, he was not totally without hope, and he knew he must try to find answers.

On March 5, 1947, Secretary Marshall and two staff members, Colonel Marshall Carter and Charles Bohlen, left for Moscow. Richard Wing, Marshall's orderly, traveled with him for the last time, because soon he would leave the Army. Marshall would need them all. Charles Bohlen was important because he had served in the Russian Embassy, was fluent in the language, and had experience as an interpreter at high-level government conferences. Marshall Carter was responsible for keeping records and paperwork straight for Secretary Marshall, and there was a great deal of paper work involved in such a conference since this was the age before computers. In addition, Richard Wing, the orderly, took care of Marshall's personal property and his arrangements.

Back in Washington, the President's speech concerning Greece and Turkey, written as a proposal and presented to Congress for approval, became known as The Truman Doctrine. Truman said, "I believe it must be the policy of the United States to support free peoples who are resisting attempted subjugation by armed minorities or by outside pressures."

Marshall did not hear the President's speech on March 12, because he was in Moscow. After reading a copy of the final draft, Marshall sent word to the President that he thought the proposal was too strong, too general, and too threatening toward the Soviet Union. Still, he did not insist on modifying the message, and he supported Truman's basic idea of providing aid to Greece and Turkey. Understanding what Truman had said in Washington, Marshall turned his attention to his first serious task as secretary of state, the Moscow Foreign Ministers Conference.

The main concern of that conference which opened March 10, 1947, was the status of Germany. After Germany's defeat in WWII, the victors divided the country into four parts, even its capital, Berlin. Now, two years later, the four nations of France, Great Britain, the Soviet Union, and the United States were meeting to agree on peace settlements. The four nations were represented by Georges Bidault of France, Ernest Bevin of Great Britain, Vyacheslav Molotov of the Soviet Union, and George C. Marshall from the United States.

Each foreign minister had aides and consultants to help with translations, writing daily memos, keeping notes, and to assist in discussions. In addition to Bohlen and Carter, the U.S. delegation included H. Freeman Matthews, a Democrat, was the director of the Office of European Affairs, and John Foster Dulles. Matthews was valuable because he had served in the State Department during WWII, dealing specifically with European assignments. Dulles, a Republican, had been an advisor to former Secretary of State James Byrnes, and had been a member of the delegation in San Francisco that established the United Nations organization. Marshall wanted to balance U.S. foreign policies that represented the views of both major political parties, so it was important to have experienced representatives from both parties.

Marshall was glad to be welcomed at the Moscow airport by the American Ambassador to Russia, Walter Bedell Smith. Smith had been one of Marshall's aides in the chief of staff office, as well as a right-hand man to General Eisenhower, during the war days. For Smith, it was a reunion of sorts with one of his former bosses, and he invited Marshall and some of his staff to stay at the American Embassy, Spaso House, for the duration of the conference.

There, the group set up the mimeograph machines and typewriters in the ballroom, created offices in the hallways and the billiard room, and made the dining room into a cafeteria. Smith wrote, in *My Three Years in Moscow*, that it wasn't long before Marshall was saying to him, 'I want you to do this and this,' and I said, 'Yes, sir,' and thought, 'Here we go again.' "

It is evident that Smith was not concerned about Marshall's ability as a foreign minister because he said, "I had seen General Marshall under all conditions of stress and strain, and I had never seen him fail eventually to dominate every gathering by sheer force of his integrity, honesty, and dignified simplicity. . . I knew he would say little until he had the situation and all the facts well in hand and that he would make no mistakes."

On March 13, Marshall commented that conducting a war was a simple profession compared to making peace. He made sure that the Soviet delegation understood him on March 14, when he defined democracy; he said that democracy insures certain rights that may not be given or taken away and these rights include "the right of every individual to develop his mind and soul in ways of his choice, free of fear or coercion—-provided only that he does not interfere with the rights of others."

Walter Bedell Smith wrote that Marshall said, "To us, society is not democratic if men who respect the rights of their fellow men are not free to express their own beliefs and convictions without fear that they may be snatched away from their home and family. To us, a society is not free if the law-abiding citizens live in fear of being denied the right to work or of being deprived of life, liberty and the pursuit of happiness." Smith says that this was "probably the most forthright statement on the rights of man ever made in Russia."

In order to have a policy passed, all four foreign ministers had to agree to the terms. During the seven weeks of meetings, they had tried daily to reach agreements. The discussions were almost useless since Molotov, the Soviet representative, refused to agree to anything except to continue discussing, which meant nothing was accomplished. Because he wanted an agreement on the future of Germany, Marshall decided to "pay a courtesy call" to the Soviet Premier, Joseph Stalin, at the Kremlin, hoping to do better with him than he had done with Molotov.

However, according to David McCullough, writing in *Truman*, Stalin asked what difference it made if no agreement was reached. "We may agree the next time, or if not then, the time after," Stalin said, as he idly doodled wolves' heads with a red pencil.

After 43 meetings, the Moscow conference finished without reaching any agreements on the status of Germany. In his many talks with Bevin and Bidault, and in what he saw and heard as he went to and from the conference, George C. Marshall decided that Joseph Stalin thought that allowing the terrible conditions in Europe to continue, without any help, would be a very good way to advance the cause of communism.

Marshall was convinced that the physical and emotional status of Europe's people was in danger as well as its economic and political situation. He was worried and troubled by the devastation he saw, and he knew the United States should and could do something to prevent the total collapse of the countries of Western Europe.

Assistance to Europe would benefit all countries, including his own. He talked at length with Charles Bohlen and Marshall Carter on the return plane trip from Moscow about the trouble he had seen and a possible solution. The United States must provide aid to Europe, in some way.

*   *   *   *   *

Monday, April 28, 1947 Marshall broadcasts his message to the people.

Man Behind the Plan

Chapter 6

A Plan in the Making

April – December 1947

Marshall arrived in Washington on Saturday, April 26 and went immediately to Liscomb Lodge in Pinehurst for the night, but he was back in Washington on Sunday evening to talk with congressional leaders. On Monday, April 28, he addressed the American public over the radio, giving a full report on the Moscow Conference.

He told the people why he was disappointed in the Moscow conference. The winter of 1947 was the worst in years for Europe and Great Britain, with waterways frozen solid. People were starving and freezing to death without food and fuel. In referring to the postwar condition of Western Europe, he said, "The patient is sinking, while the doctors deliberate." His words were a review of the speech he gave at the Pentagon in November of 1945 and a preview of the one he would give at Harvard in June.

George C. Marshall was not alone in his opinion that something must be done to help the people in Europe. While the Moscow conference was going on, Will Clayton and Dean Acheson of the State Department, Harold Stassen, Henry Wallace and Ben Cohen all worked to lay the foundation that would support Marshall's ideas of the U.S. responsibility toward helping in the European situation and recovery.

Within days of returning to the United States from Moscow, Secretary Marshall directed that the Policy Planning Staff of the State Department be activated. The staff began work in Dean Acheson's office on May 5, with Russian expert George F. Kennan as chairman. Kennan and Will Clayton, the economic expert, were particularly important in collecting the ideas that Charles Bohlen put into words for a speech that Marshall delivered at Harvard University one month later.

In early May, the Policy Planning Staff gathered information concerning the situation in Europe. The American public would soon hear about the U.S. plan to save Europe from total disaster. By mid-May, Marshall wondered where to start the State Department's campaign for a European recovery program. He had several offers to receive honorary degrees at up-coming graduation ceremonies from colleges and universities; one of those places might be a good starting place.

Harvard University had offered George C. Marshall an honorary doctorate-of-laws degree in the two preceding years, but Marshall had declined both times. In 1945, he refused because WWII was still in progress and he would not accept honors while the war was still on, and in 1946, he had been in China. The president of Harvard University, James B. Conant, had notified Marshall in February that he was again invited to receive the honor. After considering the alternative schools and exchanging letters, Marshall made his decision. On May 28, he wrote to President Conant.

Marshall told Conant that he would come and would "be pleased to make a few remarks" and "perhaps a little more." Marshall's memo to Carter on May 30, said: "Prepare a draft for a less than ten-minute talk by me at Harvard for the Alumni. . . The substance of the talk might be reference to the extremely critical period through which we are passing."

Carter sent both the study done by George F. Kennan and the information gathered by Will Clayton to Charles Bohlen, whose writing style and views were agreeable to Marshall's own. Bohlen and Kennan wrote out their ideas and Marshall wrote out some of his own. Then, Secretary Marshall talked things over with President Truman.

Under Secretary of State Dean Acheson quietly alerted the London media to listen for an important message within Marshall's address. The Policy Planning Staff and President Truman knew that Marshall was going to say something about European recovery at Harvard, but none of them knew exactly what he planned to say. Marshall was still working on the final draft, using some of their combined ideas plus his own, while on his way to Harvard in Cambridge, Massachusetts.

Harvard University Commencement, June 5, 1947

Once, over 200 years ago, in the small town of Lexington, Massachusetts that is not far from Harvard's town of Cambridge, the direction of America's development began changing with "the shot heard around the world," that began the Revolutionary War. On June 5, 1947, George C. Marshall gave a ten-minute speech heard around the world. His revolutionary words, broadcast by radio, were later known as the "Marshall Plan Speech" and helped alter the development of history.

He told the audience of 7,000 and the radio audience that it was impossible, by reading articles or looking at photographs, to grasp the real significance of conditions in Europe, "and yet the whole world's future hangs on proper judgment, hangs on the realization by the American people of what can be done, or what must be done."

He said, "Our policy is directed not against any country or doctrine but against hunger, poverty, desperation, and chaos. Its purpose should be the revival of a working economy in the world to permit the emergence of political and social conditions in which free institutions can exist. . . Any government that is willing to assist in the task of recovery will find full cooperation; I am sure, on the part of the United States Government."

In London, Ernest Bevin, Foreign Minister of Great Britain, listened to a late night news report and understood immediately that he was hearing good news for his people. Forrest Pogue wrote that Bevin considered Marshall's address "of the greatest historic significance." In reacting to Marshall's invitation, the first concerns for the European foreign ministers had to be establishing communication between the leaders of the different countries and spreading the word. Bevin later said of Great Britain, "We grabbed the lifeline with both hands."

There were requirements to meet, however, in order to receive assistance. In *George C. Marshall, a General for Peace*, Alan Saunders wrote, "The Europeans would have to overcome any distrust and dislike for one another, at least enough to communicate honestly. . . France would have to reveal to Britain what materials it lacked. The Belgians would have to talk to the Dutch, the Greeks to the Norwegians, the Austrians to the Italians——and the Germans to everybody."

Bevin wrote to Joseph Stalin that representatives from Britain and France were meeting in Paris, and invited him to send his foreign minister, Vyacheslav Molotov. Molotov came, but during the meetings, it became clear that the Soviet Union, or any country under its control, was not interested in such a plan as the U.S. government proposed. However, other countries were interested, and on July 12, 1947, representatives from sixteen nations, including France and Great Britain, met in Paris to form a Committee of Cooperation. Each of those countries would receive aid according to their needs.

Certainly, George C. Marshall was not the first to think of using American dollars for the recovery of war-torn Europe. Mark Stoler wrote, "Ever since World War I, U.S. policymakers had been emphasizing the need for the United States to take responsibility for the economic well-being of Europe as a means of ensuring prosperity, democracy, and peace." It would be economically beneficial to the United States, as well as to Europe, to do so. The U.S. had already contributed millions of dollars to certain countries, which provided no lasting results. Money was not the answer.

The plan that Marshall suggested was new and different. It said: 1) each country should define its own economic problems and suggest solutions based on those needs. 2) Each country, including Germany, must make its own plan, which must be acceptable to the other countries, before bringing it to the United States. 3) The different countries should work together for the good of each other and that the Soviet Union could be included, if they wanted to be, and 4) the plans would be completed in four years.

George C. Marshall is often called "the author" of the European Recovery Program, but he never could have written the plan alone. Marshall understood the massive need and saw the devastation, felt the United States had a responsibility to help in the repairs, and knew solutions needed finding. He gathered some of the brightest young men in the State Department, told them what he wanted done and then left them alone. The Policy Planning Staff provided the research to back up the list of needs presented by the sixteen countries, helped the European representatives outline their reports, and drafted the proposals and rules. Yet, they also had help.

Certain members of Congress were especially helpful. Marshall gained firm support from Michigan's Senator Arthur Vandenberg, head of the Senate Committee on Foreign Relations and from Congressman Christian Herter who organized the fact-finding trip to Europe. Charles A. Eaton, majority leader of the House of Representatives Foreign Affairs Committee, Dean Acheson, newly appointed United Nations Representative and Robert Lovett, who replaced Acheson as the Under Secretary of State, strongly supported Marshall's efforts, and their support was critical. Many others in various departments of the government worked on the ERP. Convincing Congress, as well as the American public, of the necessity for such a program, and for billions of taxpayer dollars, would not be easy.

Alan Saunders wrote, "Next, Marshall had to sell the plan to Congress. The price tag was high, for he was asking for $17 billion and wanted a commitment for the full amount up front. In the end, a budget of $5.3 billion was approved for the first year . . . thanks to

Marshall's tireless prodding, the European Recovery Program was launched."

It was not an easy task; it took months of committee work, research, and planning. Marshall went before congressional committees to speak for the ERP, to give facts and figures and reasons, even as he had done before the war when trying to raise the level of U.S. defense. In addition, as always, he told the truth. He convinced Congress the ERP would work and that it would benefit the United States as well. Once that was done, he went on to the next problem.

In August, Secretary Marshall attended the Latin American Foreign Ministers conference in Rio de Janerio. South American countries were in economic trouble also, because Europe was not importing their products and raw materials. Secretary Marshall had to tell the Latin American delegates that he was sorry, but the United States could not provide a "Marshall Plan" for their countries in addition to helping Europe. However, he assured the delegates that the European Recovery Program would benefit their national economic health. Marshall's honesty and friendliness helped soothe the disappointment, and his encouragement helped them plan for the treaty which they would prepare and sign at the next conference in Colombia the following year.

World problems concerned George C. Marshall and he worked to solve some of them through the General Assembly of the United Nations. As Secretary of State, Marshall was the official head of the U. S. delegation to the U.N., but President Truman appointed a former senator from Vermont, Warren Austin, as head of the U.S. delegation in Marshall's absence. Since Marshall was frequently out of the country at other conferences, his assistants from the State Department, especially Dean Rusk and Under Secretary Robert A. Lovett, and representatives appointed by Truman went to meetings in his place. Marshall kept up to date on U.N. happenings through Austin, Rusk, and Lovett.

The United Nations General Assembly began its second year in September 1947, and the meetings were the first in which Marshall participated. The subject of discussion, the partition of Palestine, was of great importance; the problem of dividing Palestine had started even before World War II ended, and it was not an easy one to solve.

The Jewish people wanted to take part of Palestine for building their homeland and becoming a new state called Israel, but the Arab people did not want to have their land taken away. The problem went to the General Assembly for negotiation. The discussion on the division of Palestine continued through the summer of 1948, and George C. Marshall was involved in those discussions. Marshall feared that if the United States backed the Jewish people and took sides against Palestine, there would be trouble. He agreed with President Truman about the idea of dividing Palestine, but he hoped the United Nations could solve the problem.

Mrs. Eleanor Roosevelt, wife of President Franklin D. Roosevelt, was a member of the United States U.N. delegation and, according to McCullough, said, "I don't happen to think that military men are particularly fitted for civilian jobs of that kind. But as far as a military man could shed his militarism, General Marshall did in the period that he was Secretary, and in the way that I saw him, which was purely as the leader of the U.S. delegation in the General Assembly, I have always had the greatest admiration and the assurance that there was no greater patriot or truer servant of his country than General Marshall."

That statement proved true repeatedly. In late November of 1947, there was another Council of Foreign Ministers Conference, this one in London, and of course, Marshall went. Before the meetings began, he was welcomed in London by some of his wartime associates, including Sir Winston Churchill. He was given an honorary doctor of civil law degree by All Souls College of Oxford University and he was invited for luncheons and dinners, with one personally hosted by King George VI.

General Marshall went to London knowing he would spend many hours in meetings trying to reach an agreement between Britain, France, the Soviets, and the United States on the subject of Germany. The conference began on November 25, and, as he had done in Moscow, Vyacheslav Molotov of the Soviet Union once again clashed with the national representatives: Ernest Bevin of Great Britain, Georges Bidault of France, and George C. Marshall. After seventeen stormy sessions, when it became clear that Molotov would not agree to anything, refusing all proposals made by others, Secretary Marshall moved for an adjournment of the meetings. The conference ended December 16 with no agreements made.

On December 17, Marshall went to say farewell to Ernest Bevin, and to thank him for hosting the conference. Bevin talked to Marshall about a vague plan he had in mind, which he described to Marshall. None of the countries in Western Europe felt safe. The Soviet forces in the eastern part of Germany had more military strength than all of the other countries had, and he asked what Marshall thought of the plan. Could the United States help?

According to Ed Cray in his book, *George C. Marshall, Soldier and Statesman*, Marshall had no specific answer ready. The only strategy he could suggest was to form a military organization somewhat like the economic grouping that would soon be presented to Congress — the European Recovery Program. That conversation was the first of many that would eventually develop a firm plan and be called the North Atlantic Treaty Organization.

The basis of the NATO agreement said that an attack on any one nation within the group would be an attack on all. By 1949, NATO included ten countries in Europe plus the United States and Canada. Years later, Marshall told his official biographer, Forrest C. Pogue, that he was pleased he had "stirred up things" and took part in starting NATO and selecting the first of its military leaders.

NATO may be the best idea that came from Marshall's trip to London. The foreign ministers conference there failed even worse than the earlier Moscow conference. When it ended, Marshall was worried and came home convinced that Joseph Stalin and the Soviet Union would do nothing to help the countries of Western Europe regain economic or political security. Marshall was disappointed and angry, yet more determined than ever to make the European Recovery Program a successful reality.

On December 18, 1947, after three long and tiresome weeks, George C. Marshall flew back to the United States, after a brief stop in Washington, went straight to Liscombe Lodge to rest, and spend the Christmas holidays with Katherine. His first year as Secretary of State had been eventful and somewhat stressful. He was glad to have a few days of peace and quiet at home, as well as celebrate his 67th birthday on New Year's Eve.

* * * * *

January 5, 1948

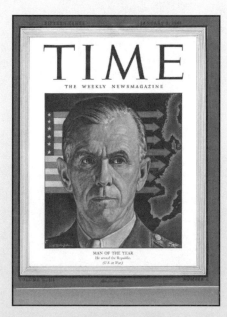

January 3, 1944

Man Behind the Plan

Chapter 7

Unexpected Support

January – March 1947

Early in January and back in Washington, Secretary Marshall was ready to start his second year in the State Department. His schedule filled up quickly, and he started the year making headline news. The January 5, 1948 issue of *Time* magazine carried his photo on the cover, as the "Man of the Year" for 1947.

During the years, Marshall's likeness was on five different *Time* covers. The January 3, 1944 issue had his first "Man of the Year" (for 1943) cover, and the magazine article declared, "In a general's uniform, he stood for the civilian substance of this democratic society. He had gained the world's undivided respect."

The "1947 Man of the Year" cover showed a portrait of Marshall backed by the wings of an eagle, with the caption, "Hope for those who need it." The article about Marshall called him " . . . a homely, reassuring man with compressed, unsmiling lips, a man who was curiously unimpassioned and unimpressive when heard on the radio. As Chief of Staff of the Army, he had established a reputation for brilliance. Congressional representatives and others who dealt with him in Washington also knew him as a man of stubborn, unswerving honesty— a good man." Newspaper, radio, and magazine publicity helped Marshall in his crusade for the ERP, and he needed all the positive coverage possible. He was concerned that six months had passed since his Harvard speech and the ERP was not yet in place. He was never one to seek publicity for himself, and was sometimes embarrassed by too much attention, but he welcomed chances to publicize the ERP.

He continued to hope that the ERP would begin within the year, but its progress in being enacted was discouraging. The lengthy congressional process was frustrating, even though he knew it had to be that way, and he did all that he could to help. The Boy Scouts of America gave his spirits a boost one day, as well as bringing more publicity for the ERP.

The Boy Scouts of America is an organization for boys age 11 and up, and the first level of Scouting is Cub Scouts, for boys in the first to fifth grade. One day in February 1948, seven members from Cub Scout Pack 232 of Bethesda, Maryland came to see George C. Marshall in his office at the State Department.

Marshall greeted them in a business-like manner, and Robert Keith Linden made the opening statement, "We are proud and happy to have met you and we want to do everything we can to help the children of Europe." George C. Marshall said, "That is a fine speech, and you said it all in one sentence."

In a letter dated March 16, 1997, Robert K. Linden, the only grown-up Scout responding to queries, told this author, "Since I was the speaker for the group, I had to read a statement in front of everyone including a group of photographers. This was the most difficult thing I had ever done in my life and it was not enjoyable until it was over."

Linden also wrote, "We were proud to help others less fortunate than ourselves by our participation in the Marshall Plan, although as children we did not really understand the full extent of the damage done by the war and the suffering caused. . . As I look back to this time, it is certainly apparent that the Marshall Plan was a necessary and important step in bringing about the peace and prosperity we enjoy today."

The Washington Daily News carried the picture and an article that said Linden's father, Keith Linden, a secretary to Representative Cecil King (D- California), and another father, Edwin Dove, the News photographer who took their picture, were with the Cubs. The fathers thought the boys should consult with Secretary Marshall about their idea before they decided to do it. For once, Marshall welcomed a photographer, and often told the story of their visit, especially during his ERP campaign speeches to the public.

Cub Scouts Walter A. Johnson, Willis W. Reeder, Paul F. Schmid, Irving Tucker, Robert K. Linden, Ronald E. Dove, and Donald F. Sheller confer with Secretary of State George C. Marshall about their Junior Marshall Plan. *(Washington Post)*

The boys, aged nine to eleven, in their navy and gold uniforms, shiny-clean faces, and slicked-down hair gathered around Marshall at his desk to explain their plan. Their picture, with Secretary Marshall, appeared in issues of the *Washington Post,* Washington's *The Evening Star, The New York Herald-Tribune* and *The New York Times* on February 11, 1948.

The Scouts called their idea a "Junior Marshall Plan" and wanted to sponsor a fund-raising event. The profits would pay for CARE packages to feed eight hungry boys in Europe for a year. The boys would be using a Roy Rogers movie, "My Pal Trigger," plus cartoons. Cowboy movies were always exciting and Roy Rogers never failed to catch the bad guys. They would charge fifty cents admission for parents and twenty-five cents for children. George C. Marshall was a fan of western movies, too, and he took the idea seriously. He was definitely impressed.

He told them: "I think it is so impressive for a group of boys of your age to undertake to provide food for a year for a number of starving children in Europe. It is a generous and fine action on your part for those children who are in dire need of such help. And it (the ERP) is of real international importance to this government in establishing a basis of friendship and good will and trust that is so important to our people and to our world and to peace."

He also told the Scouts a few stories from his days at age nine or ten and claimed he knew very little of geography or of other cultures when he was their age. He congratulated them on their efforts and wished them well, saying, "I wish very much that I could have had something like this in my record as a boy."

That same month, the Senate Foreign Relations Committee gave its unanimous approval of the ERP legislation draft and sent it on to the full Senate for debate. Marshall was a willing and well-informed witness when testifying during those three months of congressional hearings. He presented figures and facts on the problems in Europe, prepared by George Kennan and his able staff, ready for any committee's questions. Marshall's comments and opinions were important, and he was convincing and relentless in his battle for the ERP.

In addition to appearing in congressional hearings, Marshall went on a major public relations campaign, giving speeches across the country to key groups of civic leaders, men's and women's groups, farmers, factory workers, and wealthy businessmen. He traveled coast to coast drumming up support for the ERP, explaining the whys and the wherefores, the sum and substance of it all.

He told Forrest C. Pogue, "I worked on that (ERP) as hard as though I was running for the Senate or the presidency. That's what I am proud of, that part of it, because I had foreigners, I had tobacco people, I had cotton people, New York, Eastern industrialists, Pittsburgh people, some of them good friends but (all) opposed to the idea, the whole West Coast, going in the opposite direction, [and] up in the Northwest. It was just a struggle from start to finish, and that's what I'm proud of — that we put it over."

Like a Thumb in a Dike

"Putting it over" included helping the Truman administration in convincing the American public that besides being useful to the U.S. economy and the recovery of European countries, the ERP was valuable tool in the battle against communism.

It was March 13, 1948 when the U.S. Senate passed the Economic Cooperation Act by a vote of 69-17. Afterwards, the House of Representatives voted 329-74 to accept the proposed plan. Secretary Marshall was at a conference of Latin American states when he happily heard that Congress had passed the ERP. On April 3, 1948, President Harry S. Truman signed the legislation of the European Recovery Program, known everywhere as the Marshall Plan.

George C. Marshall did not use the name "Marshall Plan," because he did not think one person (himself) should receive credit for the success of something so many people helped to create. The initial idea to the finish, it took a great deal of teamwork, guidance, and patience, and George C. Marshall was definitely the man behind the plan. Clearly, Marshall did not do it alone, yet without him, it might not have happened at all.

**April 3, 1948, President Harry S. Truman signs the legislation
for the European Recovery Program.**

Andrew J. Goodpaster, writing in the *New York Times* (Dec. 11, 2003) said, The true heart and genius of the Marshall Plan was that it gave the people of Europe hope, restored their pride and delivered on the promise of something better. It proposed that the countries of Europe . . should tell the United States what they deemed best to meet their needs — not the other way around." Such a theory should perhaps be put to use today. Today our world could use the wisdom and patience of George C. Marshall. He traveled the world in planning for peace, always with compassion and the best interests of all people in mind.

* * * * *

Man Behind the Plan

Chapter 8

The Power of Balance

April – December 1948

In late March of 1948, Marshall went to his second conference for Latin American foreign ministers, the Ninth International Conference of the South American States, in Bogata, Columbia. The Central Intelligence Agency (CIA) warned him that serious trouble might be brewing in Bogata. The U.S. Ambassador to Columbia said Communists and South American left-wing liberals wanted to sabotage the conference in order to embarrass the Columbian government, and create difficulties among the South American republics while Secretary Marshall was there.

In spite of the CIA's warning of possible trouble, Marshall refused to change his routine, or his method of business, and arrived in Bogotá on March 29. Katherine did not travel with him this time, and as it turned out, it was good that she did not go. Instead, Averell Harriman, President Truman's representative, and General Marshall Carter of the State Department staff, Sergeant C.J. George, Marshall's aide, and Major Vernon Walters, his translator, went with him.

Once there, Secretary Marshall traveled by car every day from the house where he stayed to the American Embassy near the capitol building. He did his daily paper work until time for the sessions to begin, and then, with his interpreter, Walters, he walked through the streets to the building where meetings were held. Along the way, storekeepers and shoppers always recognized him, and some asked for his autograph. Marshall appeared relaxed, sometimes speaking in Spanish and exchanging greetings with the Columbian people. Things were fine for about ten days.

The violence broke out on April 9, not long after the conference began. One of Columbia's most active left-wing leaders was shot and killed in the street. Angry crowds quickly formed and the fighting began. It seemed a revolution was underway. Government buildings in central Bogotá were burned and rebels took over all eight radio stations. Mobs roamed the street and gunfire was all around. In the two days of uprising, more than a thousand people were killed.

The Columbian Army had fewer than 600 soldiers and no immediate reinforcements. Some of the conference delegates were frightened and wanted to leave, or have Secretary Marshall send for American troops. He refused to do either, saying, "It is a Columbian problem and they will have to take care of it."

At night, while soldiers surrounded the house where the American delegation was staying, Secretary Marshall sat in the living room and read a western paperback novel. His calm attitude helped to settle the delegates' fears and kept the spirit of the conference alive. The delegates voted to continue the meeting in spite of the fighting in the streets.

Marshall soon noticed the riots were disrupting local businesses. Grocery stores and restaurants closed leaving many conference delegates as well as the American Embassy staff members without food for themselves or their families. The Columbian army was so poorly equipped that the soldiers guarding him were without proper uniforms, or rain gear, and the weather was rainy and cold. General Marshall called the U.S. Army Command in the Panama Canal Zone and requested food for the dependents and 4,000 raincoats for the Columbian troops. Reinforcements were coming in from warmer areas of the country and he figured the extra coats would be needed. President Truman quickly approved the order, and the requested supplies were sent without question.

During the weeks spent in Bogotá, Secretary Marshall helped improve U.S. ties with the countries of South America. At the end of the conference in late April, Marshall was among those signing an agreement called the Pan-American Union, which eventually became the Organization of American States, a regional group of countries within the framework of the United Nations. Marshall left Bogata before the conference adjourned and was back in Washington once again, by the first of May.

Years later, Robert A. Lovett, and even Marshall himself, often told the story about the ordering of the raincoats, and food supplies (including baby food) from the Army. It seems the Army totaled up the cost of the items sent from Panama to Bogotá and eventually sent a bill to the Secretary of State. Marshall got the bill, looked it over and decided it was not a State Department cost, but should be paid for by the American Red Cross. He sent the bill back to the Army. When the Army sent the bill to the Red Cross, a year or so later, George C. Marshall was then its president. When he received the bill there, he decided it really was an Army bill, and the Department of Defense should pay it, so he sent it back to the Army with that suggestion.

By the time the bill reached the Defense Department, guess who was Secretary of Defense — that's right, George C. Marshall. He looked at the tattered and torn bill that had made the rounds of departments and decided the Defense Department would just have to pay it, finally. The paper was too old and worn to send the bill back to the Army again.

In early May, President Truman had a birthday and George C. Marshall sent him this special birthday greeting: "I want you to know that I am keenly aware of the remarkable loyalty you have given me. In return, I can only promise you to do my best and assure you of my complete loyalty and trust in you." At a private party, George C. Marshall offered a very special toast to the President, even though Marshall did not usually pay public compliments to those with whom he worked. In his toast, he said that Truman never made decisions "affecting policies beyond our shores" that were not in the best interest of this country.

Later, Marshall might have reworded that toast. The division of Palestine and the establishment of a homeland for the Jews in a new state, Israel, was one of Truman's major objectives. It was also one of Marshall's few conflicts with President Truman, and it became a tough one.

Politics entered into Truman's reasoning of whether or not the U.S. should recognize Israel. Marshall hoped that the United Nations would assume responsibility for the Palestine problem, and he felt that Truman was wrong to favor partition and recognize Israel as a separate country mostly because of United States politics.

He feared that a partition of Palestine could start another war, with the Arabs turning to the Soviets and the Jews depending on the U.S. for support. He warned President Truman that there would be continuous trouble in years to come if the United States backed Israel. Marshall's concerns have proven correct.

However, the American Jewish organizations and the officials of Israel pressured the President, and argued that the Jewish voters in America expected Truman's support of Israel. Many factors were at work; secrecy and miscommunication were two of them. The President did not fully inform Marshall of his talks with the Jewish representatives, while Marshall's opinions against supporting the partition for political reasons caused his disagreement with President Truman.

At the end of one stormy meeting, Marshall said that if Truman followed the advice of his special counsel (Clark Clifford) to support the establishment of Israel, and if he (Marshall) were to vote in November, he would vote against the President. Because he trusted and depended on Marshall a great deal, that remark was a harsh blow to Harry S. Truman.

Marshall might have changed his opinion later, but at that time his mind was made up, and he rarely changed his mind, once he decided. George C. Marshall was not a politician, and never voted in an election, because voting meant taking sides. He said that he worked for all the people, not just one group, and could not take sides.

Nevertheless, George C. Marshall worked for the President, he was a cabinet member, he was part of the Truman team, and he was loyal to his leader. Publicly he appeared to support Truman's decision on Israel, despite his own opinion. A president has a constitutional right to make a decision for the nation, in spite of an advisor's conflicting, strongly-worded, opinion.

Marshall's support, even when he intently disagreed with Truman, was a source of great comfort and strength to the President, especially during that election year. Some of Marshall's backers thought he should resign from the State Department because of his conflicts with the President on the Israel–Palestine subject. Marshall is said to have told them that one does not resign

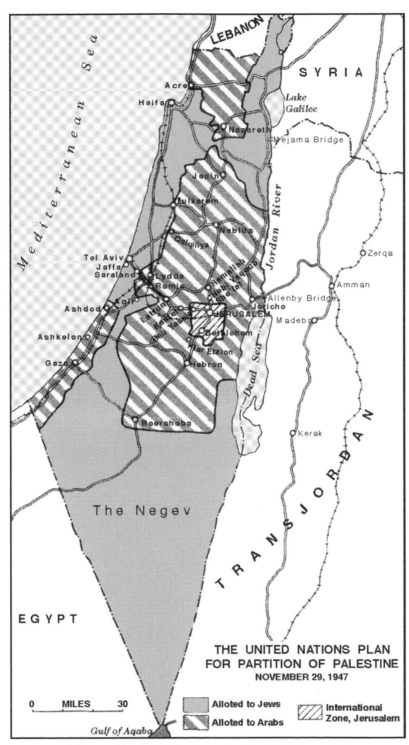

THE UNITED NATIONS PLAN
FOR PARTITION OF PALESTINE
NOVEMBER 29, 1947

Alloted to Jews

Alloted to Arabs

International
Zone, Jerusalem

Map contributed by Larry I. Bland, Editor of the
Marshall Papers, George C. Marshall Foundation

his cabinet post simply because one does not agree with the President. Friends can disagree, especially about politics, and still remain friends.

In June of 1948, both General and Mrs. Marshall went to Walter Reed Army Hospital for complete, three-day, physical checkups. Mrs. Marshall checked out in fine health, it seems. But according to Rose Page Wilson, Colonel Marshall wrote that he only had a check-up, "so that the doctors would have a full medical history on him, and in case he ever got sick they would know what he didn't have." Instead, his doctors found out what he *did* have. He had a bad kidney.

His right kidney was enlarged, there was a cyst, and doctors suggested surgery. Marshall said he did not have time for surgery and, if it were not an emergency, it would have to wait. So the doctors agreed to monitor his condition and see what happened. Marshall was confident that everything would be all right. He had other concerns about which to worry.

Toward the end of June, trouble was brewing in Germany. The Marshall Plan was becoming active at that time. Because of the Marshall Plan and the determination of the British and the Americans to reorganize the economy in the occupied zones of Germany, and to issue a new type of currency the Soviets wanted to put pressure on the Western Powers. Beginning on June 23, 1948, they created a blockade of Berlin; they closed the roads, railways, and rivers going into and out of the city.

The blockade caused trouble for the Allies because there were British and American troops and their families living in the occupation zones of Berlin. The Soviets could not control the airways, however. Since Britain and the U.S. had a written agreement on air routes to the city, the Allies began the Berlin Airlift that lasted from June 1948 until the next May, as a response. For 321 days, the Allied planes flew, day and night, from England and France for 277,264 flights. The planes carried four tons of food and supplies every day to the 2,500,000 people in the U.S., British, and French zones of Berlin.

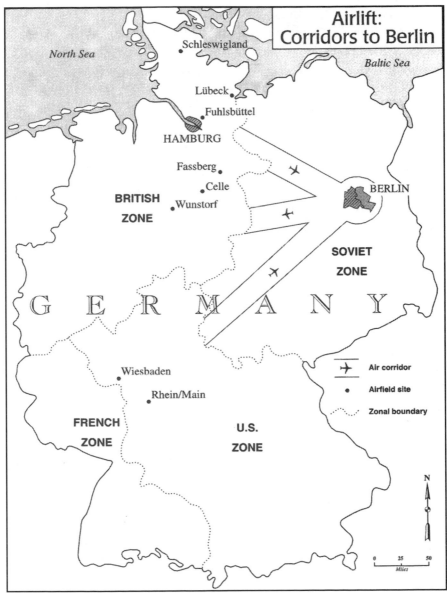

Map contributed by Larry I. Bland

During the Berlin Airlift, George C. Marshall worked to keep the Allies firmly united. He volunteered to help negotiate a settlement through the United Nations, if the blockade stopped. Marshall was a strong supporter of the U.N. and spent considerable time trying to balance problems between the State Department and the United Nations, but sometimes he had personal problems to balance, too.

That summer George C. Marshall's loyal mentor, and one of his few close friends, General John J. Pershing, died. In World War I, General Pershing was the leader of the American Expeditionary Forces and Marshall served as one of his staff officers in France during that war. After the Great War ended, John J. Pershing was named General of the Armies, becoming the highest-ranking officer in U.S. history and George C. Marshall was his aide.

Over the years, General Pershing followed Marshall's army career closely and was proud of his various accomplishments. While Pershing was in Walter Reed Hospital, Marshall visited him regularly, even when the older general was too ill to respond. General Pershing died at age 88 on July 15, 1948, and is buried in Arlington National Cemetery in Arlington, Virginia.

In September of 1948, a break in location and routine came for George C. Marshall when he traveled to Paris for the third session of the General Assembly of the United Nations. The problems before the General Assembly included the Berlin Airlift and the increased need of military and economic aid to Greece. This time Katherine went with him and they combined business with pleasure and stayed until after the U.S. presidential election in November.

During their stay in Europe, they traveled through several countries. For one, they visited Athens, and met with the King and Queen of Greece. Marshall talked to the royal couple and members of the Greek Cabinet, as well as with the British and American ambassadors and military commanders. Then he sent back to the U.S. Army, by way of the State Department in Washington, his recommendations for changes that would help the Greek army.

Queen Frederika never forgot the concern shown for her country by George C. Marshall. In the following years, the two leaders corresponded on a personal level. Now and then, Queen Fredrika asked for his advice on the problems of Greece, and he shared her letters with others in the State Department, even if he sent advice. She later visited General Marshall at Walter Reed hospital, and at his home in Pinehurst.

When November arrived, so did the presidential election in the United States. The 1948 election was a surprise victory for Harry Truman, over Thomas Dewey, allowing him to continue as president for another four years. It was not without some excitement, as the early returns so heavily favored Dewey that first-edition newspapers were printed showing him the triumphant winner. Of course, they had to be replaced.

George C. Marshall sat in Paris with John Foster Dulles and Warren H. Austin, members of the American delegation to the U.N. General Assembly, as the returns were reported by radio. Two photos of the three men show Dulles and Austin changing from elation, thinking Dewey had won and they would be receiving new jobs, to disappointment when they realized that Truman was actually the victor. Marshall's thoughtful and serious expression did not change between pictures.

Marshall's backing may have helped win the election for Harry Truman even more than the Jewish vote, on which Truman had depended. Truman's Democratic Party won control of both houses of Congress, and that meant Marshall's nonpartisan status was no longer necessary to get foreign policy items passed by the Congress.

George C. Marshall was one of America's best Secretaries of State. He was both military and civilian minded, cautious and bold, but did not promise more than he could deliver. He was non-political, having neither an agenda nor ambition for personal glory. George C. Marshall worked hard for two years representing the President to the other countries of the world. Most of all, he was loyal to his commander-in-chief during the difficult two-year period, and it was with reluctance that Truman accepted Marshall's resignation, which became final on the same day as the president's inauguration —— January 20, 1949.

Both of the Marshalls hoped the election had settled one thing for him, for sure. Retirement time had finally arrived. Marshall would resign his position as Secretary of State in January, as Truman's presidential term began, and they both would get on with their plans.

"Katherine has been counting the days," he said, ". . . until I can settle down to a normal life with her at Pinehurst and Leesburg." That was what they both hoped for, as they headed home again. This time it almost happened.

* * * * *

64

Madame Chiang Kai-shek and Katherine Marshall
at Dodona Manor, December 1948

Man Behind the Plan

Chapter 9

New Hat Number Two

December 1948 – June 1950

George C. Marshall was home from Paris by Thanksgiving and decided he might as well have the kidney operation he had postponed in June. On December 7, 1948, the seventh anniversary of the attack on Pearl Harbor and the beginning of World War II, at Walter Reed Army Hospital, Dr. Clifford Kimbrough removed Marshall's right kidney. Thankfully, the cyst that caused the problem was not cancerous, but the healing process was painful and took much longer than he had expected.

Although Marshall wanted to get to Pinehurst before Christmas, Dr. Kimbrough did not release him until almost January. Katherine kept a close watch on him and visited every day. George worried as much about Katherine's health as she did about his. He was concerned partly because she had to entertain an important visitor by herself, while he was in the hospital. At least, Katherine brought the visitor to see him.

The visitor, Madame Chiang Kai-shek, visited the United States frequently, and would stop by Dodona Manor for a visit with the Marshalls. The two women became good friends in 1946, when the Marshalls were in China, and remained so by exchanging visits and letters. They exchanged gifts at times. Once Madame Chiang gave the Marshalls some pure silk living room draperies, the kind that could not be purchased in America, and Katherine returned the favor by giving Madame a shiny new floor polisher, with extra brushes. That might sound odd, but at that time, a floor polisher was as rare in China as full-length, pure silk draperies were in Leesburg.

Madame Chiang was fond of both Marshalls. She called him 'General Flicker' (Flicker was his childhood nickname) and often wrote him personal letters, reporting to him on the changing conditions in China, throughout the years. That December she was quite concerned about the general's surgery and recovery.

As a young girl, Madame Chiang was educated in the U.S. and in later years kept an apartment in New York. She visited the States sometimes for medical treatment, and she must have received fine care because she outlived both of the Marshalls by many years, dying in 2003 at 106 years of age.

After the inauguration of President Truman, and his resignation, Marshall was able to travel to Pinehurst, but he was still sore from the surgery and not healing quickly. President Truman decided what the Marshalls needed was extra warmth and sunshine, so he arranged for them to spend time at the U.S. naval base in Puerto Rico in rather elegant guest quarters. That was a warm and welcome change.

From there, the Marshalls went to Mardi Gras in New Orleans to visit one of Marshall's VMI roommates, Leonard Nicholson. They stayed in Nicholson's guesthouse until springtime was near, and George C. Marshall was feeling better. At least, they were doing some of the traveling they had planned for in the fall of 1945.

When they returned to Leesburg in the late spring, it was time for George C. Marshall to work on his vegetable garden. He had no time to waste. Some neighbors asked Mrs. Marshall what they could give General Marshall as a welcome-home gift, and she told them he would really appreciate a load or two of good quality manure to spread in the garden. It was soon delivered, and that pleased everyone.

By the summer of 1949, just as Marshall was beginning to enjoy his retirement, President Truman was working on how to keep Marshall in the public eye and busy again. The American Red Cross was preparing to change presidents, and it was Truman's responsibility to appoint the new president. He thought Marshall would be a good choice. The job would fit Marshall well; it did not have the heavy burdens of the past eight years, but it would certainly keep him busy and put him in touch with the public again.

Four years earlier, as General Marshall prepared to retire from the Army, Truman suggested the Red Cross as a new career for him. At the time, Marshall felt the need for some R & R (rest and relaxation) after six years of worrying over war. He talked it over with

Katherine and they agreed it would be interesting work, but they did not want to commit to anything at that time. Of course, he ended up going to China for a year instead, which had not been exactly rest and relaxation.

The American Red Cross, in general, was suffering from unhappy field workers and disgruntled officers. It was in need of Marshall's special talent for staff organization and morale building, as well as his peace-seeking character. He could have just held the position, done nothing at all, and the Red Cross would still have benefited from using his name. However, that was not a George C. Marshall approach. He was almost sixty-nine, and not in the best of health after the kidney operation, yet he went to work with great enthusiasm, as if he had never before served his country.

The entire organization of the Red Cross, from administrators, workers, to volunteers needed to make some changes and George C. Marshall helped make them. With him as president, they won back some of the confidence the public had lost in the Red Cross, had fewer disagreements about local fund drives and within regional offices, and the Blood Bank promotions and volunteer recruitment were more successful.

Marshall's presidential appointments always brought many letters and telegrams of congratulations, but his selection as American Red Cross president brought the most of any. People were delighted to have him in the position, which President Truman announced on October 1, 1949. Nobody in the world was more qualified for the job.

Pogue wrote, "Favorable reaction from the military was not unexpected, but the outpouring of support from both older and younger leaders showed how wise Truman's choice had been. The only obvious regrets came from Marshall's very close friends who felt he should be taking the retirement to which he was entitled. That a man of Marshall's caliber was willing to accept this duty gave an extra touch of importance to an important cause, and made people more willing to join in the work."

As both Army Chief of Staff and Secretary of State, George C. Marshall traveled thousands of miles to make contact with the workers and the leaders. During the war, General Marshall regularly visited army drill fields, maneuvers, and bases to talk with the

**General Marshall traveled around the country
visiting Red Cross volunteer centers.**

troops and slip away unnoticed by commanding officers. He could
have "made more of a splash," as some officers thought he should
have, but he was not looking for personal recognition. He was looking for problems that needed his help.

When he was Secretary of State, he liked to talk with the people
he represented and those who worked for him, not only with world
leaders. The same was true with the Red Cross. He visited the different city headquarters and field directors, local chapters and volunteers to find out how things worked, or failed to work. He said,
"I made a quick trip around the country by airplane to look into the
Red Cross setup and meet the principal workers in 15 cities. I flew

some 7,500 miles in six days and met with the leaders of 158 chapters."

Although he had not changed his mind about keeping a low personal image, he had to admit the value of publicity. While campaigning for the European Recovery Program Marshall had learned how to use the radio to spread his message, talk to reporters, pose with "the local people," and stand still for photographers. He made contacts with leaders in various places and positions of civic organizations, farmers and business groups, and religious organizations. He told them of the Emergency Relief Fund, and the need for volunteers and donations. By June of 1950, with the coming of the Korean War, he spoke of the new Blood Bank program, and the needed support for the U.S. troops and their families. Because they knew him, when he came to talk about the American Red Cross, the people listened. Organizational problems began to improve for the American Red Cross.

On June 25, 1950, North Korean troops began invading South Korea, while General Marshall, as president of the American Red Cross, was attending an ARC board of governors' meeting in Detroit. The Korean War brought changes to the duties of the new and improved Red Cross, but it also brought a third change in the retirement plans of George and Katherine Marshall.

* * * * *

George Marshall and President Truman together again,
considering the world situation.

* * * Man Behind the Plan * * *

Chapter 10

What, Another New Hat?

July – September 1950

President Truman and his daughter, Margaret, visited the Marshalls at Dodona Manor on the Fourth of July, 1950, and it was a pleasant, social visit. However, Truman later confessed that he mainly wanted to see how George C. Marshall was feeling and if he was strong enough to take on another new job. He had hopes of bringing Marshall back into governmental action again soon, and he did.

George C. Marshall was not surprised. Rose Page Wilson quoted one of Marshall's July 1950 letters to her, writing, "Most confidentially, I have been trembling on the edge of being called again into public service in this crisis . . . (Korean War) but when the President comes down and sits under our oaks and tells me of his difficulties, he has me at a disadvantage. . ." When duty called sincerely, George C. Marshall always answered in the same way.

In August, following ten months of strong and concentrated work for the American Red Cross, George C. Marshall took a vacation. He and Katherine went to Huron Mountain, a resort in Michigan, to rest and do some fishing. Their cabin at the resort was restful, especially without a telephone.

One day he had a summons to the local country store because the President of the United States wanted to talk to him on the telephone. The people in the store milled around and stared at the tall, elderly man that some whispered was the former Secretary of State. They did not hear much from Marshall's side of the conversation except, "Yes, Mr. President."

Truman did not ask for much that day, only that Marshall stop in to see him the next time he was in Washington. Since June, and the start of the Korean War, Marshall had become more aware of the disagreements going on between the staffs of the Defense Department and the State Department.

On September 6, after returning from Michigan, Marshall paid the requested visit to Harry Truman. It did not take long to learn that Truman wanted him to be the Secretary of Defense, help with the rearmament of the U.S. troops, and get the country through its next crisis. Of course, he knew that Congress would have to approve the appointment.

Marshall was hesitant, but not surprised. Truman wrote to his wife, Bess, on September 7, 1950 "General Marshall came to see me yesterday. I told him what I had in mind. He said, 'Mr. President, you have only to tell me what you want, and I'll do it. But I want you to think about the fact that my appointment may reflect upon you and your Administration. They (Congress) are still charging me with the downfall of Chiang's government in China. I want to help, not hurt you.' Can you imagine anyone else saying that? I can't, and he's one of the *great*." Marshall was afraid that accepting the appointment might stir up political quarrels among the Congress members.

Marshall agreed to take the job on the condition that he would keep it for only six months to a year. He also requested that Robert A. Lovett, his long-time friend and colleague be given the job as Deputy Secretary of Defense, because he wanted Lovett to succeed him.

Although Truman's appointment of George C. Marshall won strong support in the Cabinet and in Congress, some decided to question it. Senate hearings followed the nomination because, even though the Democrats controlled Congress, there were those who questioned the appointment and approval was not as speedy as it had been for his Secretary of State appointment. Politics entered the scene when the Senate Committee on Armed Forces met.

Most members of the committee wanted a quick confirmation for Marshall, but Senator Harry P. Cain of Washington and Senator William Knowland of California, both Republicans disagreed. They raised the point that Marshall was still in the Army and could not be confirmed unless the National Security Act was amended. The NSA, passed in 1947, stated, "A person who has within ten years been on active duty as a commissioned officer in a regular component of the armed services shall not be eligible for appointment as Secretary of Defense." That certainly included General George C. Marshall.

After that, the committee chairman reported that Senator William Jenner, a right wing Republican from Indiana, had submitted a list of questions for General Marshall to answer. Another Republican, and a former governor of Massachusetts, Senator Leverette Saltonstall, said they should go into executive session for the questions, but Senator Lyndon Johnson of Texas said that questions presented in open session should be answered in open session. So they were.

During the questioning, Marshall sat at one end of the long table and Jenner at the other. Senator Jenner's questions were difficult ones for Marshall to answer quickly. Several had been asked or answered by others in earlier hearings, such as explaining his whereabouts on the night before the Pearl Harbor attack in1941. Still, Marshall stared calmly at Jenner and answered the queries,

Marshall listens to questions from Senator William Jenner, September 1950.

74

President Truman calls General Marshall out of the field of Retirement.

firmly and in detail. Afterwards, the committee went into executive session and approved Marshall's nomination by a vote of 10-2, with Knowles and Cain voting against him. That was only the beginning.

The debate on amending the National Security Act happened in both houses of Congress on September 15. In the House of Representatives, it was proposed that the exception to the amendment be limited to General Marshall. From the House, that proposal went to the Senate where it was accepted. Then Marshall's nomination had to be approved by the entire Senate.

Senator Harry F. Byrd of Virginia spoke in favor of the amendment and in support of Marshall. He spoke of Marshall's sense of duty and lack of personal ambition. Most of Marshall's opponents simply did not want a military man leading the Defense Department. Some spoke out against the whole Truman administration and especially against Secretary of State Dean Acheson. When Senator Jenner gained the floor, he attacked Marshall in a loud and ugly voice.

Forrest C. Pogue wrote, "In the most memorable words that he would ever speak, Jenner thundered: 'General Marshall is not only willing, he is eager to play the role of a front man for traitors... The truth is this is no new role for him, for General George C. Marshall is a living lie.' It was tragic, he concluded, that Marshall was not enough of a patriot to tell the truth, "instead of joining hands once more with this criminal crowd of traitors and Communist appeasers, who, under the continuing influence and direction of Mr. Truman and Mr. Acheson, are still selling America down the river.'"

The Senate was used to hearing heated accusations and emotional speeches, but Jenner was worse than most, that day. Then, Leverett Saltonstall stood and spoke in support of George C. Marshall. He said, "I wish I had the vocabulary to answer the statement that General Marshall's life is a lie, because if ever there was a life spent in the interest of our country, a life that is not a lie, it is the life of George C. Marshall."

When George C. Marshall heard about Jenner's speech, his comment was, "Jenner? Jenner? I do not believe I know the man."

The Senate voted to approve Marshall's nomination on September 12 and on September 15, 1950 George C. Marshall was sworn in as Secretary of Defense, at the Pentagon, by Felix Larkin. The majority of the country was glad that he was in charge of the Defense Department. Yes, indeed, General Marshall was back to work at the Pentagon, again.

Mrs. Marshall accepted her husband's decision to once again pour himself into the stress and strain of decision and policy making on behalf of the armed forces with some concern, but she knew he had to do what he felt was right. Maybe if it were only for one year, it would be all right.

William S. White, of the *New York Times Magazine* wrote about Marshall wondering why he would leave the peace and quiet of Dodona Manor to rejoin the chaos of the world. One reason was that Marshall "could not close his eyes" to the troubles between the State Department and the Defense Department. White decided the demanding days ahead might be of concern to Mrs. Marshall, but not to her husband. "The General is a man of toughness and of realism so profound that the fact of deep hostility to him held by many is treated in his mind exactly as the fact that there are a certain number of miles, some of them on narrow, uneven roads, between here (Washington) and Leesburg."

There were indeed "rocky roads" to cover and several fences to mend between Cabinet members, the Joint Chiefs of Staff, the State Department, and the Defense Department. Only George C. Marshall served as both Secretary of State and Secretary of Defense. His strength of character as well as his administrative leadership served both departments well. Differences of opinion between the Secretary of State Dean Acheson and the former Secretary of Defense, Louis Johnson, had kept the two departments at war with each other, but George C. Marshall could mend that fence easily.

Secretary of State Dean Acheson followed Marshall as head of the State Department. Acheson was confident of Marshall's support and wisdom and secure in their separate positions. They were united in purpose and he often went to the Pentagon to meet with Marshall. The two had worked well together when Marshall was his boss and they knew each other's methods of operation and basic ideas. Pogue said that as "an instinctive matter of courtesy," Marshall arranged for regular conferences between Acheson and himself and between their staffs.

Pogue wrote, "He knew life on both sides of the river (the Potomac) having directed the building of the Pentagon as well as the original part of the building occupied by the State Department. No one had to tell Marshall to stop the feuding and fussing between the Departments of State and Defense. The "State" of things just naturally improved once Marshall was back in the Cabinet. His presence sent a clear signal to all involved that defense and foreign policy were working together, as a team, again."

The U.S. armed forces were not ready for another war, but Marshall knew how to fix that problem, too. He needed first-rate assistance, and knew where to find it.

* * * * *

The four leaders; Marshall, Eisenhower, Truman and Acheson appear to agree on their plans.

**Secretary of Defense Marshall and Secretary of State Acheson
making staff plans, September 1950.**

Man Behind the Plan

Chapter 11

Carrying Through

September 1950 – May 1951

The Cold War that began in 1947 turned into a hot war in June of 1950, and by the time Marshall took office in September, was well underway. George C. Marshall went straight to work and, during his one-year term as Secretary of Defense, he dealt with three critical and connected issues, all having to do with the Korean War.

The United States, as part of the United Nations combined forces, was heavily involved in the defense of South Korea. North Korean troops, backed by the Soviet Union, invaded South Korea, and the U.S. was called on for help.

The number and strength of U.S. military forces had dropped drastically in the five years since the end of WWII. Troops and military equipment were needed in Korea, so Marshall's first task was rebuilding the armed forces. Stoler wrote, "Building an army was nothing new to him. Indeed this was the third time he had undertaken such a task." His experiences from WWI and WWII made this task routine.

George C. Marshall said, "I was getting hardened to coming in when everything had gone to pot and there was nothing you could get your hands on, and darned if I didn't find the same thing when I came into the Korean War. There wasn't anything."

Marshall helped restore confidence in the Department of Defense and to make clear the direction the armed services were to proceed. Marshall made sure that his assistants, his staff, the Joint Chiefs of Staff, and the secretaries of the armed services understood his basic views on international security and national defense. They also knew he disliked secrecy and intrigue, demanded simplicity in plans, brevity in reports, insisted on a clear chain of command, and believed in responsibility and loyalty up and down that chain. Also

Marshall felt that the State Department outranked the Defense department, and he did not like unnecessary formality.

At that time, the chairman of the Joint Chiefs of Staff was General Omar Bradley, one of the five 5-star generals of WWII, a Marshall protégé as well as one of the "Marshall Men" from the Fort Benning days of 1930. George C. Marshall was happy to work with Bradley again, and said that had he been asked to choose a chairman for the JCS, Bradley would have been his choice. Others on the JCS staff were the Army Chief of Staff General J. Lawton "Lightnin' Joe" Collins, General Hoyt Vandenberg, Chief of Staff of the Air Force, and Admiral Forrest Sherman of the Navy.

Pogue wrote, "At the first conference between the service secretaries and their staffs, Marshall carefully placed himself on the civilian side of the table across from the admirals and the generals." In this way, he sent a signal to those involved, that the Defense Department and the State Department would work together and that the administration was in charge of the military as well as the civilian side of government.

It was soon clear that Marshall did not intend to work alone; he needed talented help. As in each of his previous jobs, he found able assistants, delegated authority to them, and left them alone, trusting them to do the best job possible.

Robert A. Lovett, Marshall's Under Secretary of State, who had left government work when Marshall left the State Department, in January 1949, came back as the Deputy Secretary of Defense. Marshall and Lovett were kindred spirits. They thought alike and approached problems systematically, without letting personal emotions interfere. They even agreed when they disagreed. When Marshall was out of the country and a decision needed making, Lovett could make it and it would be exactly what Marshall would have done. Lovett was his right hand man and Anna Rosenberg became his right hand woman.

Marshall asked President Truman to nominate Mrs. Anna M. Rosenberg as Assistant Secretary of Defense for manpower and personnel. Mrs. Rosenberg had an impressive resume from WWII days, knew about army manpower, and was a member of the Advisory Board on Universal Military Training. Both Dwight D. Eisenhower and Walter Bedell Smith were friends of hers. Marshall valued their

opinion and knew they valued her work. In fact, Eisenhower rec-
ommended her for both the Medal of Freedom in 1945 and the U.S.
Medal of Merit in 1947, which she won.

Truman agreed with Marshall's choices. Lovett needed no
approval by Congress, just Marshall's invitation, but Anna
Rosenberg was a different story. Not long after Marshall took office,
she came to Washington to discuss her position on the staff. He
warned her that his opponents in Congress would probably attack
her nomination. After all, she was a Jew, a New Yorker, and a
woman. Being a woman trying to fill a position normally held by a
man was the hardest obstacle to overcome.

Robert A. Lovett, Marshall's right-hand man, Deputy Secretary of Defense

She suggested they wait until after the November elections so that her appointment would not be used against Truman's administration in the voting booths, and so they did. It was December 14 before the Senate voted and approved of her nomination.

Mrs. Rosenberg said later that Marshall kept coming into her office that day and asking if she had heard anything. He had a meeting in progress in his office with the Joint Chiefs of Staff, but asked her to interrupt them when she heard the results, regardless.

Pogue wrote that Anna Rosenberg said, "When I got word, I rushed in. He and the Joint Chiefs had their coats on, I was choked up. He said, when I told him I was confirmed, 'That's good. Go home and get a facial; you look like hell'. The Joint Chiefs looked shocked that General Marshall would know anything about a facial."

In January of 1951, Rosenberg and Marshall testified in Congress as to the need for Universal Military Training. Legislation was passed that extended the draft for four more years, lowered the draft age to eighteen and a half, increased the period of active duty to two years, and added a six-year term in the inactive reserve. Pogue said that Anna Rosenberg snowed Congress with a blizzard of accurate manpower statistics and astute estimates, but it was June before Congress adopted the principle of UMT for the first time in U.S. history, and they never did pass a bill to establish permanent UMT. Rosenberg went to work to rebuild the U.S. armed service manpower, but the rebuilding of the military forces for the Korean War had to be done without UMT.

With the draft law in effect, U.S. forces doubled in number during the year Marshall served as the head of defense. One of the five-star generals from World War II, General Douglas MacArthur, was already in Japan as he had been while Marshall was Secretary of State. The Joint Chiefs of Staff awarded the U.S. Far Eastern Commander, General MacArthur, the immediate control of all military forces in Korea, as well.

Deciding on how to handle the Soviet Union and Communist China and how to reach a cease-fire were difficult political decisions for the U.S. government. Thirteen other countries had armed forces in action in South Korea. Together with the U.S. forces, they made some headway in defending against the Communist forces. In early

**Anna Rosenberg sworn in as Assistant Secretary of Defense,
December 1950.**

1951, Marshall and Acheson worked with the United Nations for a
cease-fire in Korea. Planning the strategies and the purposes of U.S.
policies in Korea was a combined effort of the President, Secretaries
Marshall and Acheson, and the Joint Chiefs of Staff. Each department had its say, but the President was the Commander in Chief. A
cease-fire and settlement was not easy to find, even though the U.S.
government was working through the United Nations.

The efforts of the JCS, the State Department and the Defense
Department were not enough. The fighting increased, the
Communist troops outnumbered the U.N. armies, and South Korea
was in danger. Because he tended to be critical of the Truman
Administration and the U.N. policies, General MacArthur was told,
in November 1950, to clear any public statements he made concerning the war through the President's office. Yet, in March 1951, he
wrote to Joseph Martin, the Republican leader of the House of

Representatives, strongly criticizing the U.N. approach and the letter was made public.

Instead of waiting for the political cease-fire through U.N. negotiations, MacArthur decided it was time to increase the pressure on North Korea and China. He wanted to advance across the 38th Parallel, the dividing line between North and South Korea, and attack in China. Secretary of State Acheson wanted Marshall, as Defense Secretary, to stop MacArthur by ordering him to keep his forces south of the 38th Parallel.

Into and throughout March, the situation became worse. Tough decisions had to be made, and eventually, the U.S. focus was compelled to center on General MacArthur, who was allowed to freely direct the forces under his command as he saw fit. He grew more confident of his own tactics, and feeling restricted in his freedom to attack, he ignored the restrictions set up by President Truman.

The more freedom MacArthur used, the more the governmental storm clouds darkened in Washington. The news reporters began to wonder who was in control of the United States policies— the government or MacArthur. President Truman answered that question in early April.

Truman decided to bring MacArthur out of Korea. He wanted to be sure his action was justified, so he asked George C. Marshall, Dean Acheson, and General Omar Bradley for advice. Because MacArthur had a long and impressive history of command and the American public admired him, Marshall, Bradley, and Acheson urged the President to use caution in his reaction and to take a weekend to consider the alternatives and the possible public reaction. Politically, it was a risk for Truman to dismiss him.

On Monday, April 9, 1951, the President met with Marshall, Acheson, Bradley, and Averell Harriman and Pogue reports, "All political and military leaders consulted by the President concurred in his decision." He quoted Marshall, "With the unanimous concurrence of all those present, the President at that time took his decision to relieve General MacArthur."

President Truman issued this statement. "With deep regret I have concluded that General of the Army Douglas MacArthur is unable to give his wholehearted support to the policies of the United States Government and of the United Nations in matters pertaining to his official duties. In view of the specific responsibilities imposed upon me by the Constitution of the United States and the added responsibility which has been entrusted to me by the United Nations, I have decided that I must make a change of com-

Traffic Trouble

mand in the Far East. I have, therefore, relieved General MacArthur of his commands and have designated Lt. Gen. Matthew B. Ridgway as his successor."

General MacArthur's dismissal occurred because he had been "unable to give his wholehearted support to the policies of the United States Government and of the United Nations." Mainly, because he refused to listen to the President, General Douglas MacArthur was recalled from his post and retired from the army. In other words, he was fired.

Some people blamed George C. Marshall for MacArthur's dismissal. The two generals were not overly fond of each other; they had their differences, and had crossed paths for more than forty years. Marshall was not happy to see MacArthur dismissed from command, but he understood why it happened. MacArthur, alone, was at fault.

MacArthur was offensively conceited and self-important, and never admitted doing anything wrong. Still, Marshall saw beyond MacArthur's excess behavior and regretted the outcome it caused. He told Rose Page Wilson that, "he considered it a tragedy that vanity 'brought down' a man who was a real military genius." Marshall helped arrange the public military welcome given MacArthur when he returned to the States. He made sure that transportation to Washington was available for MacArthur's former staff members, and was among the first to greet MacArthur at National Airport in the first hour of April 19, 1951.

Pogue wrote, "Public . . . reaction against Truman and his chief advisers, Acheson and Marshall was bitter. . . A few old Army friends turned against Marshall and some of his fellow VMI graduates, who had served with MacArthur, strongly condemned him. Yet the country's most respected military leaders supported the power of the Commander in Chief to dismiss a powerful general who opposed presidential policy and the constitution."

Following MacArthur's dismissal, there were Senate hearings to explain the recall, beginning on May 3, 1951. The Senate Foreign Relations and the Armed Services Committees questioned those involved in the problem. Several committee members, both Republicans and Democrats, backed the President's action, but not all of the twenty-six members of the investigating committees did. Douglas MacArthur had loud support from the listening crowds and many Republican congressional members.

MacArthur testified first, for twenty-three hours in three days. His testimony made clear that he was mainly interested in fighting a war centered in the Pacific-Asian half of the world. Cray wrote, "To the end, he protested his innocence and his loyalty to the chain of command. To the end he insisted that the president, a civilian, had meddled in the conduct of the war, not that he, a soldier, had tried to set national policy. . . and he insisted he did not know why he had been relieved."

Then General Marshall took over, and the senators heard a different story. The concerns of the United Nations and the United States were of global proportions; the issues and solutions included the whole world, not just Asia. He explained the problems with expanding the war into China and the possibilities of starting a third world war. He made sure the committees understood that any soldier, from private to general, must obey orders from their commander, even when they disagree with the order. By the time the hearings were finished, two months later, it was clear that President Truman had done the right thing. General Matthew B. Ridgway replaced General MacArthur in Tokyo. General James A. Van Fleet took command of the Eighth Army in Korea on April 14, 1951.

Marshall Day at VMI, May 15, 1951

Man Behind the Plan

Chapter 12

More Ups Than Downs

May 1951 – September 1951

With the MacArthur problem behind him, Marshall took time to visit his alma mater, Virginia Military Institute, for his 50th class reunion, along with thirty-six of his classmates in mid-May. He had visited the school several times since his graduation in 1901. He was there in 1920, when he brought General of the Armies John J. Pershing to speak to the cadets, after World War I. Marshall was a VMI football star during his senior year and he had visited for Homecoming or football games, enjoying his visits to the Barracks and the Mess Hall, or watching the cadets on parade.

Twice, in 1940 and 1950, Marshall had delivered the graduation address at VMI. Rose Page Wilson wrote, "The interesting thing is that his opening words on both occasions were identical: "This is a day of high emotion for you men; it also might be one of the most fateful days in the history of the world." [In 1940, the Germans were advancing on Paris, and in 1950, the North Koreans were attacking South Korea.]

His 50th reunion became a most special day, because this time he, and not the cadets, was the honored guest. On that day, VMI was dedicating a new archway to the Barracks. The other two arches, already named for famous generals, were (George) Washington Arch and (Stonewall) Jackson Arch. The newest one, named for VMI's most famous graduate, became the (George C.) Marshall Arch on May 15, 1951 as the Institute celebrated *Marshall Day*.

That day Marshall also received the Commonwealth of
Virginia's Distinguished Service Medal, presented by Governor
John S. Battle. Marshall's friend, Bernard M. Baruch, was the speaker for the archway dedication, addressing a large audience that
included Virginia's governor, members of the Virginia General
Assembly, and members of Congress, cabinet officers, and military
leaders among others.

When Marshall responded, he talked about some of the cadet
graduates he had seen during his years in the service. Larry I. Bland
wrote in *Fully the Equal of the Best*, "Knowledge of specific academic
fields or even of tactics or strategy were not the Institute's most
important products, Marshall asserted; rather they were character,
integrity, dependability and acceptance of responsibility in a
crisis. . . The next day he told an old friend that the dedication 'was
a big day in my life, for VMI paid me a great honor. . . The day was
perfect in all respects.' "

A few weeks later, on June 5, Secretary of Defense George C.
Marshall "slipped away from Washington" and went to Korea to
see for himself what the war situation was. This was General
Marshall's last visit to an active war front, and he said the situation
was worse than he had expected. During the Korean War, 29,557
service members died in battle, or from battle-related injuries, 4,184
died from non-combat causes, and 7,245 became Prisoners-of-War.
Many of the wounded were treated at a *Mobile Army Surgical
Hospital*, or battalion / regimental first-aid stations, and returned to
duty, but 92,934 seriously wounded were treated at a M.A.S.H. and
evacuated from Korea.

One of the most popular of all television series, beginning as a
movie in 1970, was *M.A.S.H.* The program, based on a novel by
Richard Hooker, had Korea as its setting and war situations as its
theme. It provided plenty of entertainment and laughs, even as it
illustrated the frustrations, fears, and futility of war.

Marshall returned to Washington on June 12, and met up with a
personal kind of war, a verbal attack by the first-term senator from
Wisconsin, Joseph McCarthy. In April of 1950, McCarthy had called
George C. Marshall "completely unfit" and "completely incompe-
tent," and in December had demanded that he be removed as
Secretary of Defense. The recent MacArthur upheaval had only

**General Marshall in Korea with General Matthew Ridgeway
and General James Van Fleet, June 1951.**

increased McCarthy's bitterness and anger toward Marshall, and
the attention and honor paid to Marshall by the state of Virginia
and VMI only added fuel to McCarthy's fire.

McCarthy announced that he would speak, which he did for
almost three hours, in the Senate on June 14. The galleries were full
of listeners, but many left before he finished, as did all but two senators.

McCarthy had assistance from Forrest A. Davis, an editorial
writer for the *Cincinnati Enquirer*, who wrote a lengthy, anti-
Marshall, and skillfully crafted document of misinformation. The
partial quotes were taken from writings done by Churchill, Mark
Clark, James Byrnes, and Admiral Leahy, who all admired Marshall.
Pogue wrote, "He (Davis) or members of McCarthy's staff, lifted
statements out of context, added comments in quotations that were
not in the original, omitted qualifying sentences, . . .and cited as fact

unproved charges made from various hearings." Later, the State Department found the real and complete statements taken from the writers cited, which praised George C. Marshall instead of condemning him as the cut and spliced together Davis article did.

McCarthy changed what Davis wrote a bit, claimed he wrote it, and read it poorly, as his speech. He had the 60,000-word article placed in the *Congressional Record*, and stopped just short of accusing George C. Marshall of treason. He claimed that Marshall's career was "steeped in falsehood." He later published the article as *America's Retreat from Victory: the Story of George Catlett Marshall*, sent it to daily newspapers around the country, and distributed it in Wisconsin Schools.

Of course, newspaper reporters rushed to query Marshall and get his reaction to the McCarthy speech. Cray wrote, "When Clayton Fritchey offered material for a rebuttal, Marshall declined politely. " I do appreciate that, but if I have to explain at this point that I am not a traitor to the United States, I hardly think it's worth it."

In her book, Rose Page Wilson tells of a conversation she had with "Colonel Marshall" in Washington. She asked why he would not confront McCarthy publicly and defend himself. She wrote, "Colonel Marshall shrugged off my suggestion and remarked that aside from the fact that he always steered clear of politics, clean or dirty, would I really want him to demean himself by exchanging words with McCarthy? I told him no. . . but it was frustrating that he wouldn't make a single public rebuttal. . . "If I did that, I would acknowledge something that isn't true, that McCarthy's accusations are worthy of defense. There is no necessity for me to prove my loyalty to the United States; I have lived that loyalty every day of my life."

Although Joseph McCarthy verbally attacked others, even the president, he did not harm George C. Marshall in the long run. The United States Senate reprimanded McCarthy for his actions in December of 1954 by a vote of 65-22.

In the summer of 1951, George and Katherine needed a change of scene and a fresh outlook so they took a trip to Cape Cod. They had the use of a friend's vacation home on a point known as Waquoit. In the house next door was a six-year old boy named Corty, also on vacation, visiting at his grandmother's house.

Corty went next door to visit with the owners of the house where Marshall was staying, and was surprised when a stranger, a tall man with gray hair and a wide smile, appeared at the door. The two struck up a friendship and discovered they both liked to fish. Eventually, the older man went fishing with Corty and his family. Corty caught the most fish of all. Later he sent General Marshall a letter decorated with pictures of fish with real fishhooks attached. According to one source of Corty stories, (John Gunn, of Lexington, Virginia) George C. Marshall decided to fill up some potholes in the driveway using wet seaweed. He and Corty loaded the seaweed into a wheelbarrow. Corty earned ten cents an hour to ride on top of the seaweed, from the beach to the road, and keep it from spilling from the wheelbarrow.

After the Marshalls went home, another Corty story says that one evening at dinner, he told his mother and grandmother that he saw his "very good friend" on television. He was reminded that

Pinehurst, N. C.
12/14/51

Dear Corty: I was surprised and delighted to get your Xmas
card. It was very clever and you are quite an artist as well as
a famous fisherman. I only wish we could go out again and raid
the blue fish in their den. That rhymes but doesn't make much
sense.

I have been shooting this fall. Got 2 turkey, 18 pheasant
and a good many quail, all on an island off the Georgia Coast.
We are going again Xmas week for quail in South Carolina with
a Mr. Baruch and then we may go to Mexico or to far off New
Zealand and Australia in the Southwest Pacific, and on to South
Africa (get out your book and check up on this). The government
of New Zealand invites me to be their guest including all of the
most famous fishing in the world that I care for. But I don't think
we will go.

Give my warm regards to your Father and Mother, your grand-
parents and your family. For yourself my love and affection.

signed/ G. C. Marshall

Any recent contracts for hauling seaweed?

telling fibs was not a good practice. Still, Corty insisted that he had seen his good friend and planned to write him a letter. When his grandmother asked which one of his friends he thought he had seen, Corty said the General from next door. His grandmother then agreed that indeed he probably had seen his "very good friend," George C. Marshall, and that if he wanted to write him a letter, he certainly could. Corty did write a letter, complete with colored pictures and real fish hooks.

For a number of years, Corty's letter was on display at the George C. Marshall Museum in Lexington, Virginia. This writer, being interested in the child behind the letter, tracked down Corty, and talked with him by telephone. He says that he considered General Marshall "a dear friend," kept the letters that he received from him, and has an autographed photograph hanging on his wall. He still vacations in Waquoit, but now has three sons of his own to help him fish

A year to the day after he was sworn in, on September 12, 1951, George C. Marshall announced at a morning staff meeting, "At eleven o'clock I cease to be Secretary of Defense." He told them that he had planned to stay only six months, but the President asked him to stay on until June, then until September because a new crisis always came along making no time a good time to go.

He said that he had completed fifty years of government service, including the year with the Red Cross. He felt that the past year had been eventful and satisfactory, and concluded by saying that he could not take credit for the progress made in their department. He admitted he had "pushed a few things" but he was ready to "sit down and reflect and see what others were going to do."

When Secretary Marshall left, Robert A. Lovett took his place, just as planned. General Marshall Carter remained on Lovett's staff, and Colonel C.J. George would work part time for Lovett. Marshall would still have "an office in the Pentagon" including a secretary and Colonel George to handle Marshall's mail. The war continued until the United Nations, North Korea, and China signed an armistice July 27, 1953, which ended the conflict, but failed to bring permanent peace to Asia.

George C. Marshall was weary, almost seventy-one years old, and not in the best of health. His memory for names, even of those whose faces he well knew, was fading and his hearing was failing, which he found embarrassing as a public official. Katherine's health, too, was declining and she worried more than he did about the McCarthy attack. He wrote President Truman that he was resigning for "very personal reasons" and Truman responded that he accepted his resignation, with reluctance.

George C. Marshall had done more than his share for his country and its ten presidents during his forty-nine years and ten months of public service. He had traveled more than a million and a half miles as chief of staff and a cabinet officer, and he simply wanted to drive out to Leesburg and stay home for awhile. He did not know that his influence as a man of the world was still unfinished, but he knew his long-awaited retirement was about to begin.

* * * * *

Man Behind the Plan

Chapter 13

Here to There and Back Again

October 1951- May 1953

What does a career soldier and statesman do when he is no longer making plans for the nation and the world? In 1945, the Marshalls made extensive plans, but after a six-year delay, those plans had changed. At least they did not have to search for a retirement home or an apartment. They knew where they would live. Now there were new ideas to explore, and it did not take the Marshalls long to settle into the comfortable and less complicated routine of Leesburg and Pinehurst.

Their largest house and first home was Dodona Manor. In the fall of 1941, Katherine Marshall drove around the Virginia countryside in search of a place where she and the general could escape to, away from the demands of his office and the city. She found the house she wanted on the eastern edge of the small town of Leesburg, in Loudoun County, about thirty-five miles from Ft. Myer. She told the General about it, and they bought it, even before he saw it, for about $16,000. That was lot of money in 1941 when the average yearly salary was less than $2,000 and gas cost twelve cents a gallon.

The Marshalls traveled Route 7 many a time as they visited the house, on weekends and holidays. They did not want stores or offices to build close to them so they bought the extra land surrounding the house, bringing their grounds area to four acres. The main section of the two-story brick farmhouse, built in the 1820s, had been added onto through the years. There were 23 rooms, 4 fireplaces, 69 windows, and a roof painted red. Whenever and however they could get away from D.C., George and Katherine spent time at their place in the country. It needed repair when they bought it, and they started fixing it up, bit by bit, as soon as they could.

While General Marshall was in London for a few weeks in April of 1942, Katherine had the house cleaned and some major repair work done, with new paint and new trimmings both inside and out. The day he returned, she took him to see the first house he had ever owned. Having lived the army life of moving and rented quarters, he was amazed and pleased with the way the house looked. He told her, "This is home, after forty-two years of wandering." Katherine knew she had done the right thing.

The Marshalls house was named Dodona Manor, before they bought it, because of the oak trees that grew, and still grow, around it. Dodona was an oak grove in Epirus, Greece where it is said there lived a prophet of the Greek god, Zeus. Supposedly, priests interpreted the rustling of the oak leaves in the breeze as messages from Zeus himself to the prophet. Perhaps the Marshalls felt the tall trees would whisper secrets to them, also, especially about their gardens.

George and Katherine both loved the planning and the physical labor of gardening. They found it relaxing to put on their old clothes and spend time tending their very own garden and grounds. In May of 1942, Marshall planted his first garden at Dodona Manor. He wrote to his sister, Marie Singer, ". . . the place looks lovely and greatly improved. I converted a plowed and harrowed field in front of the house into a lawn, cleaning out rocks, raking it down into a fine soil, sowing grass seed and binding it in."

During the war years, especially, General Marshall enjoyed the exercise and distraction of hoeing corn, pulling weeds, and trimming bushes whenever he could escape to Leesburg. His skill as a gardener was evident in the products of his plants.

One of his staff, Lt. General Walter Bedell Smith, came one rainy day to deliver an important message, just received by telegram, from someone important and far away. He found General Marshall in the garden, picking corn. As his crisp uniform began to wilt, Smith asked, "Sir, do I have to stand here in the rain to make my report?" and his boss, pointing toward a bucket, said, "No, Smith, turn that pail over and sit down."

Marshall spent a great deal of time gardening, and he was always interested in discovering new techniques or products to improve the outcome of his efforts. His efforts at Leesburg produced the following funny story that he often enjoyed telling.

Someone at the State Department told him he could improve his garden soil and production by placing a fish head under each seed or plant, as the American Indians used to do. When he asked them about where to get fish heads, he received several baskets full on a Friday afternoon. He put them in the trunk of his car in the parking garage, in downtown D.C., but he stayed in the city and did not go home that weekend. By Monday, nobody wanted to park near his car!

He dutifully took the smelly things home and planted his seeds and tomato plants on top. During the night, he and Katherine heard a lot of "yowling," and the next morning they discovered that the stray cats of Leesburg had invaded his garden, dug up and eaten the fish heads, leaving the seeds and the new plants to wilt in the sun.

During the Potsdam conference in the summer of 1945, General Marshall was in Germany when his corn and tomatoes were ready to harvest. One day, Mrs. Marshall surprised the General, and everyone else, with fresh corn and tomatoes sent straight from his garden in Virginia to Germany. She wrote, "I was determined that George should have at least a taste of the fruit of his labor, so I got up early one morning and packed a dozen ears of corn, with the dew still on them, with a half dozen large tomatoes." She sent them in a box to the War Department and they went on the daily plane that flew the mail to Potsdam. "George wrote me that the vegetables arrived as fresh as when picked. . . They were a treat beyond words and he was a proud farmer among diplomats and military commanders."

While George was busy with the vegetables, Katherine was growing flowers, such as phlox, zinnias, August lilies, Sweet William, and roses. She grew wonderful peonies and daylilies, whose descendents have spread like a family and still bloom every year. She also had a walled patio, two rose arbors, and several winding brick walkways built for the garden. Over the years, she created a very pleasant outdoor living space.

Katherine had graduated from Hollins College in Roanoke, Virginia and had a flair for dramatics and style, as well as planning gardens. She was a gracious hostess and enjoyed serving tea or breakfast on the patio, where they often entertained guests at lunch under the whispering oak trees.

The Marshalls enjoyed entertaining their family, their neighbors, or famous friends traveling from far away or nearby. During the spring and summer of 1952, President Truman went out from Washington to Dodona Manor for a visit with his friend, George C. Marshall. They could sit under the oak trees and talk safely about matters of national or world concern. Truman would return to the White House with dependable advice, valuable information, or another interesting anecdote.

The Marshalls were not wealthy, but they were comfortably well off. In 1948, at President Truman's request, Congress passed the legislation that gave him the full salary and benefits of an active general, as they did for the four other five-star generals. Truman made sure he had adequate office space at the Pentagon, an aide, a secretary, and an orderly. He also had free air transportation whenever he needed it.

Their family was not large; it included Katherine's oldest son, Clifton Brown, her daughter, Molly, and Molly's husband, Colonel James L. Winn, and their three children, Jimmy, Kitty, and Ellene. George had no children of his own, and Katherine's younger son, Allen Tupper Brown, was killed and buried in Italy during World War II. Clifton died at Walter Reed Army Hospital of lung cancer in the spring of 1952.

With a large house to care for in Virginia and a comfortable cottage in North Carolina, it was good for the Marshalls to have dependable help. They had a maid to cook and clean, and they had Sergeant Heffner to attend to the personal needs of the general, run errands, do the shopping, drive for them, and help with or supervise the household chores and repairs.

Sergeant William J. Heffner was Marshall's last in a long line of orderlies. Bill Heffner was born and raised in Philadelphia and entered the Army in 1932, served in the 8th Field Artillery in the Hawaiian Islands and at Ft. Hoyle, Maryland. During World War II, he was a supply sergeant. He served as Marshall's chauffeur and orderly from 1945-59, and when he retired in 1960, he received the Certificate for Outstanding Performance by the U.S. Army Service Center for the Armed Forces in recognition of his 27 years in the Army. Sergeant Heffner died April 12, 1995, at age 86.

Starting in 1951, Sgt. Heffner did all the driving for General and Mrs. Marshall. When Marshall needed to go into DC for the day, they would drive to a service station in Dranesville where they would change from the Marshalls' own Oldsmobile to the Cadillac provided for Marshall by the government. General Marshall did not like to be seen arriving at, or leaving from, Dodona in such an expensive car.

Cray writes in his book, "The quiet life of a small town in the Virginia countryside delighted Marshall. He ran errands, sometimes pushed a cart through the local market to do the family shopping, or stood in line at the post office to buy stamps... Two family dogs (Bones and Nato), summoned with a piercing whistle followed him on walks."

In Leesburg, the Marshalls attended the Episcopal Church, and a few times some of his suits and coats turned up at the church bazaar. He attended Rotary meetings, and movies at the Tally Ho Theatre. He liked western movies and mystery novels, and enjoyed listening to the radio and watching television. He also read biographies and books written by his former colleagues.

Nobody knew it then, but George C. Marshall had written a book. He named his book *Memoirs of My Services in the World War, 1917 – 1918*, and submitted it to a publisher, perhaps sometime around 1927. The publisher said there was no interest in that "conflict" at the time. Of course, when Marshall became chief of staff in 1939, the publisher asked for permission to publish it. Then, Marshall said no, and had it sent back to him to be destroyed. Later, however, it was published, in 1976, after Molly Winn, Katherine's daughter, found the carbon copy he had given her in a trunk in the attic.

They both enjoyed reading and did some writing. Katherine wrote a book, *Together, Annals of an Army Wife*, published in 1946, that became a Book of the Month Club selection. Her story is full of family happenings, General Marshall's career, and their army life experiences.

Catching up on the mail

Liscomb Lodge, Linden Road, Pinehurst, North Carolina

George C. Marshall was also a prolific letter writer. He claimed a quiet spot in a Dodona Manor bedroom where he could read his mail and write his answers in longhand. Then he would send or take them to the Pentagon office for typing and mailing. Colonel George collected General Marshall's mail, sorted it out, answered some of it for him, and took him piles of new letters. He was not limited to writing in Leesburg, though; he could also write letters from Pinehurst.

The spring and summer were fine in Virginia, but when frost came, it was time to go to North Carolina. Liscombe Lodge fitted their needs well while in Pinehurst. The house, built around 1925, was not as large or as formal as Dodona Manor; it really was more of a vacation home, a place to relax, a retreat for the Marshalls. They bought it in December of 1944, six months after D-Day, and General Marshall did not see it until February of 1945. Once Katherine finished fixing it to her liking, it became their winter home. Of course, Sergeant Heffner and their maid went with them.

Katherine wrote in *Together*, "The Lodge was small and attractive and the grounds were really beautiful. George would work here surrounded by long-leaf pines and magnolia trees, with a lawn of winter grass as green as emeralds spread out before him."

It "was a modest, clapboard bungalow, set in a smallish garden and so well screened by trees that it was barely visible from the road" according to an anonymous writer.

The house is on Linden Road, almost in the center of the village. They could have walked to the Village Chapel for church and to the Carolina Hotel for Sunday dinner, but Sergeant Heffner usually drove them. Records show they donated $100 a year to the chapel and the Pinehurst Religious Association. Donations also went to the American Red Cross in Moore County, NC and Loudoun County, VA. They liked to contribute to the Pinehurst community.

Pinehurst still has many retired people, including generals, just as it did when the Marshalls lived there. Many like to ride horses, but even more like to play golf. Today there are eight or more golf courses in and around Pinehurst. Some say they play every day of the week, and on a different course each day.

George C. Marshall was not a golfer. When he first arrived in Pinehurst, in 1945, *The Tin Whistles*, an old organization of active men golfers, elected him to be an honorary member, but that did not convince him to pick up a golf club. He enjoyed watching golf matches from his Jeep station wagon, or from a campstool, with binoculars and giving a play-by-play account in very fine golf terms, to anyone close enough to hear, including Katherine, Rose Page Wilson, or his orderly, Sergeant Bill Heffner.

General Marshalll watches the golf match while Sgt. Heffner watches the golf cart in Pinehurst.

One anonymous source said that Pinehurst let General Marshall live like an ordinary person, not like someone in a glass showcase. The Marshalls often entertained their guests at the Carolina Hotel or the nearby Country Club. Their house was not large enough for big dinners, but they still joined in the social life of the town. If they went to a cocktail party, he liked to mingle and talk. He would often sit and tell stories of his long career, but always ones of a personal nature, mostly funny ones. Politics was not a subject for social situations.

There are people in Pinehurst today who remember meeting or knowing George C. Marshall. One is Bob Burwell, who owns a golf related business and whose parents were friends with the Marshalls because they were neighbors. Bob remembers, "I played with two other childhood friends on the floor of his (Marshall's) living room with hundreds of toy soldiers he owned.... (We) would set up battle lines and play war while he watched from his chair. Also, I remember walking past his house and noticing military and other important cars parked there, and being told he was being visited by foreign dignitaries. This was a common occurrence."

One of those occurrences would have been Queen Fredericka of Greece, who came with two of her children, or it could have been Lady Nancy Astor from England, Senator Adlai Stevenson, General Omar Bradley, or one of the Presidents, Truman or Eisenhower.

Billy G. McKenzie tells about standing guard at Liscombe Lodge more than once due to important visitors. McKenzie, who is more than eighty years old, was born in Pinehurst and is an admirer of George C. Marshall. Mr. McKenzie was in a group of volunteer firemen called to line the sides of Linden Road, making sure that all went well, when famous people were visiting the General. At least once, he planted himself in the perfect spot to shake hands with President Truman.

McKenzie, like Marshall, had two careers; one as a banker, and one as a locksmith. He was a Marine in WWII and has lived and worked in the area since, making more money as a locksmith than as a banker. His wife worked in the bank also and one day she saw General Marshall come into the bank, same as usual, to cash a check. The teller, Elsie Black, asked to see his identification. Mrs. McKenzie hurriedly whispered to Elsie, and the check was cashed. General Marshall only laughed.

General Marshall talks with Roady Williams on the steps
of the post office, 1951.

"Mrs. Marshall was a gracious and lovely lady," Billy McKenzie said. He was a Boy Scout Master, and one evening Mrs. Marshall called him. She wanted him to bring her grandson, Jimmy Winn, home after the scout meeting because it would be dark. He assured her that Jimmy would get home safely. When they arrived at Liscombe Lodge, she invited him to come in for hot chocolate and cookies. General Marshall joined them in the kitchen. "Mr. McKenzie," the General said, "Jimmy tells us that during Boy Scout meetings, you run a pretty tight ship. Is that true?" McKenzie replied, "Yes sir, it is." McKenzie answered. "What branch of the service did you serve in?" "The Marines, sir," to which General Marshall said, "Then, I think you and I both appreciate the importance of discipline, regardless of age."

Retired generals and admirals find Pinehurst a great spot to live. Among those, in 2004, is General Sam Sims Walker, retired four-star general and former superintendent of Virginia Military Institute, who also happens to be on the Board of Directors for the George C. Marshall Foundation. He knew General Marshall, before WWII, when Marshall was commanding general of Vancouver Barracks, Washington, and considered him a friend.

At that time, Sam Walker was eleven or twelve years old, and his dad was as an executive officer on General Marshall's staff. Walker said that General Marshall was particularly fond of his garden and the grounds around his quarters along Officers Row. "Because we lived next door, my parents were careful to keep our grounds neat and attractive. On his way home from his office one evening he saw me cutting the grass with an old push lawn mower. He was always teasing and joking with me and said, "Sam, I want you to wait a few minutes while I go get my movie camera. I won't even have to put it in slow motion. That is the slowest-motion grass-cutting I have ever seen."

As Sam's father moved up in rank, Sam grew up, also. By the time Sam was in high school, General Marshall was Army Chief of Staff, and the war was underway. One day, Sam had a Sunday afternoon date and he drove her to visit the Marshalls at Ft. Myer. The girl thought he was tricking until they stopped at Quarters One, he rang the bell, and once inside she heard General Marshall say, "Is that you, Sam? Come on up here." Sam's date was impressed.

General Sam Walker, 11th Superintendent of VMI
1981-1988

General Walker, a veteran of both the Korean and Vietnam Wars, has letters in his scrapbooks from General and Mrs. Marshall that cover his growing years and his army career. Sam graduated from West Point, as did his father. They are the only father-son set of four-star generals in U.S. Army history. Walker is happy to talk about Marshall and considers it an honor and privilege to have known him so well.

In his George C. Marshall Lecture in Vancouver, Washington on November 9, 1990, General Sam Walker said, "In this century his legacy has cast a huge shadow. Today our army bears his stamp. He built the victorious army of World War II. He forged an alliance for the free world and devised a plan to rebuild a devastated Europe. What he began would bring down the Berlin wall and lead to the disintegration of the Warsaw Pact. In the long run it could be said that George Marshall contributed to the end of the Cold War, the reunification of Germany and the reshaping of the Soviet Union."

The people of Pinehurst will not forget that George C. Marshall lived in Pinehurst. Marshall Park, a playground and open space, near the Pinehurst Country Club has a stone monument, clearly seen from the street that is decorated with seasonal flowers or with an evergreen wreath on December 31, Marshall's birthday. Mary Evelyn de Nissoff, a reporter for a Pinehurst newspaper, *The Pilot*, covered the dedication ceremony for her paper and said, "Margaret Truman Daniel came here among a handful of other dignitaries."

The Pinehurst house was sold soon after General Marshall died, and Mrs. Marshall moved away. It has passed on to other families, but can still be recognized as "the Marshall House." The Leesburg house was purchased from Katherine's daughter, Molly, and is being renovated and refurbished by the George C. Marshall International Center, and is open to the public by appointment. Years have changed the looks of the towns and the condition of the homes, but General and Mrs. Marshall had a number of good years in both places. Retirement was more pleasant because of the places they lived and the people they knew as well as the places they traveled.

* * * * *

Man Behind the Plan

Chapter 14

Off to See the Queen

June 1953 – October 1 953

The fall of 1952 brought another presidential election, and this time Dwight David Eisenhower replaced Harry S. Truman. Of course, Marshall did not vote, but he sent his congratulations in a letter he wrote in his hard-to-read longhand, "Congratulations on your triumph seem rather futile in view of the immensity of your victory. I pray for you in the tremendous years you are facing. I pray especially for you in the choice of those to be near you. . . . Make them measure up to your standards."

Marshall also wrote a note to Adlai Stevenson, Eisenhower's opponent, whom he knew well and had worked with on the ERP and through United Nations projects. He wrote, "I send you my sympathy in the results of the campaign. You fought a great fight. In my opinion, your political speeches reached a new high in states-manship. You deserved far better of the electorate and you will be recognized increasingly as a truly great American."

The Marshalls were invited to the attend Eisenhower's inauguration, the swearing in and to sit in the reviewing stand for the inaugural parade, which they did. Later, President and Mrs.Eisenhower often invited the Marshalls to the White House for special occasions, such as formal state dinners and when dignitaries from other countries were being honored. Marshall was not fond of formal dinners and parties, but he did enjoy greeting leaders and diplomats from different parts of the world. George C. Marshall was on speaking terms with many of the world's important people. He and Mrs. Marshall were helpful in making the visitors welcome.

In 1953, President Eisenhower appointed George C. Marshall to lead the special delegation, or committee, to represent him and the United States at the Coronation of Queen Elizabeth II. When King George VI, of Great Britain, died in 1952, his daughter, Elizabeth, became Queen. The British people celebrated Elizabeth's ascension to the throne, by scheduling a formal ceremony, called a coronation.

General Marshall first met King George and Princess Elizabeth while he was in London during World War II, he had been in London when she was married, and he had seen her in Washington when she and her husband, Prince Philip visited. When her father died, Marshall wrote a letter of sympathy to Princess Elizabeth, and she sent him a personal thank you letter.

Dear General Marshall,

I was touched by your kind letter of sympathy, and I do want to thank you with all my heart for your thought in writing. I know that the King very much enjoyed meeting you and I remember so well when you came here during the war. It seems impossible that he has left us—-he was so full of ideas, of plans for the future, but we shall try to carry on, as he would wish. With again my thanks to you and Mrs. Marshall for thinking of us at this time of great sorrows.

I am, yours very sincerely, Elizabeth R.

The Marshalls traveled by ship to England, sailing over the Atlantic Ocean on the *United States* and returning on the *America*. This was his first trip by sea to England since 1910 when he and his first wife, Lily, took a vacation in England. He had sailed the Atlantic twice during World War I as he traveled to France in 1917, first as a captain in the First Infantry Division with General William L. Sibert, and second in 1919, as a colonel on General John J. Pershing's staff when he returned from France. His travels overseas in World War II, while serving as Army Chief of Staff, had all been by plane. Happily, this trip was all for good will.

There is a great deal of tradition, formality, and elegance connected with a coronation. In London, royal ceremonies are traditionally held in Westminster Abbey, a large cathedral. Many countries sent their leaders, as government representatives, to pay tribute and honor to the new monarch. Only invited dignitaries, British government officials, and royal family attend the actual ceremony in the Abbey, but many are included in the festivities that follow. The Queen, of course, is the center of attention. Her crown is so heavy with jewels that it is difficult for her to wear, but she wore it briefly for the very special occasion of her coronation.

While in London, the Marshalls probably stayed at the U.S. Embassy, but on the day of the Coronation, they were at Grosvenor House, a hotel not far from where the coronation took place and the view from their room included London's famous Hyde Park. Mrs. Marshall, along with many guests, was not invited to the Coronation. She stayed at the hotel, where she had a fine view, and watched the procession of the Horse Guard, the Queen's carriage, and her family as it traveled the streets, lined with people, from Buckingham Palace to Westminster Abbey. After the Queen went by, Katherine joined the other guests for tea until it was time to watch the returning parade that followed the coronation.

For George C. Marshall, a coronation was a new experience. He had seen five Presidents inaugurated in his own country, but this was his first coronation. Westminster Abbey was full of important people as Marshall went to his assigned seat near the altar. The lengthy and solemn ceremony would be filled with music, speeches, prayers, and the Queen's proclamation. With him, among others of the delegation, was General Omar Bradley, a friend and WWII general.

According to General Bradley, as General Marshall was walking down the aisle, the audience stood up. Marshall asked Bradley who was coming in and why people were standing, and Bradley said, "They're standing for you." Marshall never mentioned that incident, but he did comment about Prime Minister Winston Churchill. "He dignified me in the Abbey by turning out of the procession to shake hands with me after he had reached the dais."

Bradley and others of the American party said that Field Marshal Bernard L. Montgomery, England's top WWII general, also stopped to greet Marshall. The British knew George C. Marshall well. He had been their friend through two world wars and the European Recovery Plan.

The happy celebration lasted several days and both Marshalls attended dinners and dances given in honor of the Queen, but General Marshall was the only one from the U.S. delegation to attend the banquet at Buckingham Palace. He said it was, "the most brilliant gathering I had ever seen. The Queen's party of thirty was

Mrs. Katherine Tucker Marshall, June 1953, wearing a gown from Razook's of Pinehurst she bought for the coronation celebration.

seated at an oval table in the center of the hall surrounded by tables of twelve." He was seated next to the Queen Mother, and two chairs away from the Queen.

Sir Winston and Lady Churchill and other prominent government members as well as the royal family entertained them. They even attended the Derby with Churchill, which must have been fun for Marshall. His favorite sport had been horseback riding. Forrest C. Pogue wrote that the Marshalls visited with "Sir Reginald MacDonald-Buchanan, whose wife Marshall thought was the sole heir to the Guinness Stout business." Marshall wrote, "They had a beautiful place about two hundred miles out of London. I think their family has had nine Derby winners and most of the portraits (in their house) were of horses." President Eisenhower certainly picked the proper couple to lead the delegation and represent the United States. George and Katherine Marshall had a 'royal good time in London' that month! However, they were ready to go home to Virginia, to Dodona Manor and their gardens.

* * * * *

The Marshalls at home in Pinehurst, October 1953

Man Behind the Plan

Chapter 15

All Eyes on the Prize

October – December 1953

The Marshalls returned from England pleased with a trip worth remembering. Unfortunately, in September they both came down with severe colds that hung on and on, for both of them, as bad colds sometimes will. Every fall they went from their Leesburg home, Dodona Manor, to Lipscomb Lodge in Pinehurst, North Carolina to spend the winter months. Since their colds were hanging on, it seemed best to go south earlier that year. The General's cold turned into influenza even as they hurried to Pinehurst in hopes of a speedy recovery.

George's cough was bad and it did not get better. Katherine worried about his condition and insisted, toward the end of October, that he go to Walter Reed Army Hospital in Washington, DC for treatment. While they were considering making the long trip by car, an invitation arrived from the White House inviting them to a state dinner honoring the King and Queen of Greece during their first visit to the United States.

Marshall would have enjoyed seeing his friends King Paul and Queen Frederika, but he called President Eisenhower and declined the invitation due to illness. When the President learned that Marshall was ill and coming to Walter Reed Hospital, he arranged for a two-engine plane to fly him there, and for him to stay in the Presidential Suite. Queen Frederika came to visit with General and Mrs. Marshall at the hospital, which both surprised and pleased him.

In his spare time, while being an impatient patient, Marshall read and answered letters. One letter went to the beautiful and gracious Madame Chiang Kai-shek. He told his friend, Madame Chiang about his illness, missing the state dinner, and especially about Queen Frederika's visit. "She is a very beautiful and most interesting woman and you might consider her 'working' royalty, as she certainly devotes all of her time and energy to her people."

He also wrote that he remembered when Madame Chiang had visited him while he was in Walter Reed in 1948, and wondered to her why it was that, " . . .whenever I receive women of this stature, I am a patient in the hospital." General Marshall admired intelligent women like Madame Chiang and Queen Frederika and he did not mind at all if they were beautiful.

Just before the Marshalls left Pinehurst for Washington, they were surprised with exceptionally good news. Word came from the Nobel Prize Committee that George C. Marshall was receiving the 1953 Nobel Prize for Peace. Marshall won the recognition for his sponsorship of, and his hard work in making happen, the European Recovery Plan, known to all as the Marshall Plan.

According to Forrest C. Pogue, when General Marshall phoned President Eisenhower to thank him for sending the plane that took him to Walter Reed Hospital, he told the President about the Nobel award. Eisenhower was delighted and congratulated Marshall, saying that he often wondered why certain people win such awards, but "this time I thoroughly approve."

Pogue wrote that Harry S. Truman, one of those who nominated Marshall for the Peace Prize, was almost beside himself in his approval, some of which he expressed in an evening (television news) interview with Edward R. Murrow, which Marshall saw by chance. Marshall wrote the former President, "I watched it with considerable interest and, as you can well imagine, was deeply appreciative of the honor which you paid me. As usual, you were most generous and kind and while the years pass into oblivion, I will never forget your unstinting support."

Sir Winston Churchill sent a telegram: "Many congratulations on your selection for Nobel Peace Prize, I am proud to be in such company for this years awards." Churchill won the Nobel Prize for Literature in 1953. Marshall would have enjoyed visiting with him in Oslo, but only the Peace Prize is given in Oslo. The Nobel prizes for medicine, chemistry, physics, and literature are given at ceremonies in Stockholm, Sweden. Winston Churchill did not get to Stockholm, due to failing health. Lady Churchill, who also read his acceptance speech for him, accepted his prize.

Marshall answered Churchill on November 16, "As to your Nobel Prize award, I thought it wonderfully appropriate. You are preeminent in many things, but especially so in your writing. You have been preeminent in everything in the past 30 years, but nothing more magnificently than in the leadership you have given the world through the medium of your compelling voice."

Concerning the Nobel Prize, Marshall's goddaughter, Rose Page Wilson wrote in *General Marshall Remembered*, "I was overcome with pride and joy. To me, this coveted and distinguished award was a superb recognition of Colonel Marshall's long, selfless service to his country and to mankind."

In a letter to his sister, Marie Singer (Mrs. John J.) in Greensburg, Pennsylvania, on November 6th he said, "I was tremendously surprised when a correspondent of the International News Association called Katherine and asked for my reaction to the award." He had no idea that the committee was considering him for the prize and so was taken off guard. Marshall told his sister "the panel which consisted of five members of the Norwegian Parliament cast a unanimous vote in my favor."

George C. Marshall wanted to share the honor of the Nobel Prize with those who helped him win it. In a letter to Dean Acheson on November 6, Marshall said, "Although the award is individual in nature, it really belongs to all the people. I hope that you will share in this distinction with me ——you did much to make it possible." He also told Truman, "I hope you will share this distinction with me because it was through your guidance and leadership that the European Recovery Plan was made possible."

The news of the Peace Prize did not cure his bad cough, but he prepared to go to Norway. Mrs. Marshall did not go with him, and she strongly felt that he should not go either, due to his lingering illness, but George C. Marshall was determined to be there in person, even though he had to go alone. He did not travel alone, though, because his aide, Col. C.J. George, went along and was invited to all the official happenings. Marshall decided they would sail on the *Andrea Doria*, the newest Italian ocean liner, and Col. George sent for the tickets, which cost about $350 each. Marshall expected to soak up some sunshine and enjoy the voyage. Surely, a sea trip would get rid of his flu virus. He also had a speech to write.

George C. Marshall thought he would have time during the eight-day voyage to rest and write his Nobel lecture, but he was wrong on both counts. He did not get well, and he did not get his speech written. His doctors thought the sunshine and warm weather of the southern route from New York to Naples, Italy might be good for his recovery. His doctors were wrong, too. The weather was cloudy, damp, and cold for the entire trip.

Later, Marshall wrote to Harry Truman, "It (the voyage) was an eight day affair and I planned to prepare my Oslo so-called lecture enroute. I found it utterly impossible to concentrate and I landed in Naples without a line" (of written speech). From Naples, he flew to Paris and stayed with General Alfred Gruenther who had taken General Eisenhower's place of command in Europe.

On the deck of the Andrea Doria, December 1953

Marshall wrote to Rose Page Wilson, "I left the boat at Naples less well off than when I started. Fortunately, I had the use of the NATO Supreme Commander's plane so traveled comfortably and fast. Every day I was in Europe, except at Oslo, I stayed in bed until dinner in the evening and did not go out at all."

Forrest C. Pogue tells us that while in Paris, from his bed, Marshall dictated his Nobel Lecture, talking for over an hour. He had help, from some of Gruenther's staff, with writing the phrases and ideas in long hand, and Colonel Andrew J. Goodpaster got down on the floor and put the various bits of paper together and then had it typed. Marshall flew from Paris to Oslo the day before the award ceremony.

Marshall spent two full days and evenings in Oslo, Norway. The directions concerning the award ceremony came through the mail from the American Ambassador to Sweden, L. Corrin Strong, who wrote, "bring white tie, tuxedo, cutaway, and dark business suit. Also suggest you bring miniature decorations to wear at Nobel Committee Dinner." General Marshall was not one for wearing his medals, but he would have to wear a few for this occasion.

Strong sent along a schedule for the Nobel events, which Marshall studied with some concern. He would have a press conference, a meeting with the mayor, three lunches, and two dinners to attend. There were acceptance speeches to give, which could be short, but he was to give a lecture that should last about an hour.

The Nobel Peace Prize included a solid gold medallion, weighing about six ounces, inscribed with his name, a certificate, and a cash award of 175,292.94 in Swedish crowns, which translated to $33,840 American money. According to a letter, among the Marshall Papers, Norges bank in Oslo sent a check for $33,792.55 to Marshall's bank in Richmond, Virginia. Most of the money went to pay off the mortgage on their house in Pinehurst. The medallion is often on display in the George C. Marshall Museum in Lexington, Virginia.

Forrest Carlisle Pogue, who would later be Marshall's official biographer, was in Oslo to witness the award ceremony. In his fourth book, *George C. Marshall, Statesman*, Pogue wrote, "On the afternoon of December 10 at the University Auditorium in the city of Oslo, the King of Norway, and other dignitaries gathered to wit-

**Dr. C. J. Hambro presents Nobel Peace Prize,
December 10, 1953.**

ness the presentation of the awards for 1953. Dr. Albert Schweitzer, the great missionary doctor in Africa, received the first award, which was given to him in 1952. In his absence, it was accepted on his behalf by the French Ambassador to Norway. Then Dr. C.J. Hambro, a member of the Nobel Peace Prize Committee, spoke about Marshall's military record and of his postwar achievements."

When Hambro finished talking, Marshall stepped forward to receive the prize, and as he reached the platform, a disturbance began in the balcony. Three young men ran about shouting, "Murderer! Murderer!" and "We protest!" "This is no peace candidate!" "Marshall, go home!" as they threw leaflets over the railing. The paper flyers accused Marshall of committing military crimes, especially in the use of the atomic bomb. The audience was surprised by this outburst, but Norway's King Haakon VII stood and started the applause for General Marshall, with the entire audience following his lead, that drowned out the shouts of the three protesters.

George C. Marshall did not panic. He looked toward the balcony, because of the noise, but he did not react. General Marshall did not seem alarmed, perhaps because he had been yelled at before. Irwin Abrams wrote in *The Nobel Peace Prize and the Laureates*, "The general turned to Hambro and commented dryly that in his own country he was more accustomed to such treatment from anticommunists."

The crew that had flown Marshall's plane to Oslo was sitting in the balcony, and they grabbed the hecklers and, helped the guards hustle them from the balcony and outside to more security guards and a waiting vehicle. Rose Wilson wrote that General Marshall told her, "The Commy business was more press than fact, except for the time required for the leaflets to fall from the balcony."

George C. Marshall appreciated the help of the Air Force men, and on December 15th wrote a thank-you note to the captain of the flight crew, Orlo V. Harkness. "I shall always remember the fine effort you made in connection with the presentation ceremonies in the University Auditorium. I know Mrs. Marshall will be very interested in hearing the story."

The disturbance did not last long. After the commotion calmed down, the ceremony continued and General Marshall received his prize. He thanked the committee and accepted the honor on behalf of the American people, saying they were the ones who deserved the credit for carrying through and finishing the European Recovery Plan.

On the evening of December 11, a formal dinner was given in his honor by the Nobel Committee in the Rococco Room of the Grand Hotel. Following the meal, General Marshall, handsomely dressed for the occasion in white tie and tails (and wearing a few of his "decorations") gave his Nobel Lecture which was open to the public. He knew there might be complaints about his being the first professional soldier to receive the prize for peace, so he addressed that issue first.

"There has been considerable comment over the awarding of the Nobel Peace Prize for Peace to a soldier. I am afraid this does not seem as remarkable to me as it quite evidently does to others. I know a great deal about the horrors and tragedies of war. . .The cost of war is constantly spread before me , written neatly in many ledgers whose columns are gravestones."

In his speech, George C. Marshall did not recommend giving up national military defenses. He said that the countries of the world were destined to need moderate military power to maintain peace, but that military strength alone was not enough. He said, "A spiritual regeneration to develop good will, faith, and understanding among nations" was a primary factor of peace, and that economic stability of individual countries, as well as a necessary balance of power between nations, was also important.

He went on to say, "And with all these there must be wisdom and the will to act on that wisdom. . . Because wisdom in action in our Western democracies rests squarely upon public understanding, I have long believed that our schools have a key role to play. . ." To study what caused the breakdown of peace in past centuries would be useful, he thought. He felt that schools, including colleges, should concentrate on teaching the causes of past wars, and he said, "Preferably our senior high schools, should have courses which not merely instruct our budding citizens in the historical sequence of events of the past, but which treat, with almost scientific accuracy, the circumstances which have marked the breakdown of peace, disruption of life, and the horrors of war."

Marshall said, "It is certain that insecurity, intolerance, and distrust all lead to war." He spoke of the ways that national leaders might bring peace to the world. He stressed the importance of compromise and tolerance, taking time to understand the problems of another country or another culture and for those in leadership roles to steer their country toward secure economic and social improvement. He finished his talk with, "I hope I have sown some seeds, which may bring forth good fruit."

Today, the seeds he planted that December night are still growing but somehow the fruit has not yet ripened. Perhaps if our present and future world leaders will cultivate the seeds of peace with patience and tolerance, the fruit will someday ripen.

Marshall was not happy with this speech, but he said he had done the best he could. He said what he meant and he meant every word. It may not have been his best speech, due to his illness and his situation while writing it, but the words and the ideas he gave in Oslo still ring true, fifty years later.

The next day Marshall and Colonel George flew to Frankfurt, Germany where he stayed with a friend, General Thomas Handy, for a few days of rest. He then chose to fly back to the states on a government plane instead of taking the *Andrea Doria* again.

George C. Marshall appreciated the Nobel Peace Prize, and his trip to Oslo, but he was also grateful to be on his way home. His trip was over, he had accomplished what he went to do, but he had not recovered from his illness.

* * * * *

The family helps General Marshall read some of his 75th birthday cards and letters.

Man Behind the Plan

Chapter 16

Home to Stay, More or Less

January 1954 - 1959

The five years following the Nobel Peace Prize ceremony were fairly quiet years for the Marshalls. They went back and forth from Pinehurst to Leesburg, depending on the season. They traveled a little, and he wrote many letters. The lengthy bout of flu and/or pneumonia in the fall of 1953 seemed to be the start of George C. Marshall's failing health. He had always believed in daily exercise, but now, even brief daily walks became an effort for him. He cut back on his speeches and appearances at various places and for civic groups. The Marshalls spent some of their traveling time going back and forth to Walter Reed Army Hospital for check-ups and treatments. They entertained small gatherings more often at home.

Whenever he went to Walter Reed, President Eisenhower made sure he was given the Chief Executive's suite. Marshall appreciated Eisenhower's thoughtfulness, as well as the extra privacy. Eisenhower was happy he could help the man who was partly responsible for his own success and the one he considered a mentor. In a letter to a friend in 1954, Eisenhower said, that of all Americans he had known personally, "I think General Marshall possessed more of the qualities of greatness than any other."

On December 31, 1955, George C. Marshall celebrated his seventy-fifth birthday at Liscombe Lodge, in Pinehurst. Sergeant Heffner took family photographs, reporters came to visit, and he and Mrs. Marshall made a short television appearance. A beautiful birthday cake was sent to him from the Pinehurst Country Club. He received telegrams, cards, and letters from hundreds of friends and well-wishers, from Sir Winston Churchill, Presidents Eisenhower and Truman, and the heads of state of free nations all around the world. Newspapers carried articles about Marshall and pictures of him at home, in retirement. They referred to him as "the architect of victory," "a selfless patriot" and "the greatest living American." Of his seventy-five years, at least fifty had been in active service to his country.

From the day of his retirement in 1945, Marshall had been encouraged to write about those years of service — his army career, and his years in government work. Marshall said that he could not write an autobiography, telling his own story, without telling the truth. He knew the truth might embarrass or hurt certain people and he did not wish to do that. Several publishing companies offered him high prices, up to a million dollars, for his life story, but he flatly refused.

Marshall said he had never kept a diary of his actions during World War II or later. He felt writing down daily happenings would be limited by the fact that somebody would read them, or they might be used as evidence in investigations. If he did not write the facts the way they happened, he would have to change them in some way, and that would be wrong. Moreover, it would take time and energy away from concentrating on the business at hand and getting his job done.

However, in mid-1956, the prospect of getting someone else, perhaps an experienced historian, to write Marshall's biography began to take shape. Mr. J. Clifford Miller, then vice-president of the George C. Marshall Foundation, wrote to Forrest C. Pogue, a World War II historian, who was teaching history at Murray State University in Kentucky. Miller offered Pogue the job as director of the new George C. Marshall Research Center at the Foundation and a chance to be the official interviewer of General Marshall. Pogue was excited about the idea, but he was cautious about giving up his teaching position, and spent time asking some tough questions, first.

Pogue visited with Colonel C.J. George, General Marshall's aide, at the Pentagon, and talked about getting access to the Marshall papers. President Eisenhower had renewed President Truman's order of 1953, which made available, as far as possible under government regulations, all of Marshall's official papers to the director of the Marshall Research Center. In addition, Colonel George had already talked to Brigadier General Frank McCarthy and Major General Marshall S. Carter, former Marshall aides, about getting Marshall to talk to an historian, and they had mentioned their choice, a man by the name of Forrest Pogue. Plans began to fall together.

**Forrest C. Pogue, Marshall's official biographer,
in the George C. Marshall Research Library**

Pogue heard that Marshall had finally agreed to be interviewed about his career, for an authorized biography. Haste was important, though, because Marshall was not in the best of health. Colonel George told Pogue that someone had asked what they could give Marshall for his seventy-fifth birthday, and Colonel George had suggested a tape recorder. Pogue knew the modern device of tape recording would be a wonderful help and a time saver. He would not have to take hurried notes as Marshall talked, but could talk slowly with him, replay the tapes, listen and then write.

Frank McCarthy along with John C. Hagan, then president of the Marshall Foundation, talked with Forrest Pogue. They wanted Pogue to stay three years at the Foundation, and he said if he did that, he would have to be the full-time, official, and total biographer. After some more consideration and talk, it was settled. Forrest C. Pogue would be the official biographer for General George C. Marshall.

In August of 1956, a few days after the Marshalls returned to Leesburg from a northern vacation, John C. Hagan and Colonel C.J. George took Forrest C. Pogue to meet General Marshall. Pogue reminded the general that he had witnessed the Nobel Prize ceremony in Oslo, and they had exchanged letters. With that, the ice was broken, according to Pogue; they soon were talking and making plans for working together.

Marshall's first concern was that no biography would be published before he died. Second, if a biography were written, no money would come to his family, but would only be used for research studies. Finally, he wanted the interviews to start soon, and it is a good thing they did.

General Marshall came to his Pentagon office a few times but was more comfortable working at home, so Pogue went to him, at Dodona Manor or at Liscombe Lodge, and put the tape recorder to work. The reel-to-reel recorder was awkward at first, but Sergeant Heffner took charge and helped the General. He even hung the microphone above his head, so Marshall would not have to hold it while talking. That cut down on the noise a great deal.

Pogue had been prepared, from the start, with about a hundred questions he had wanted to ask General Marshall for several years.

Sometimes he would ask the questions in person and sometimes he mailed Marshall a list of questions. Often, Sergeant Heffner would read the questions, Marshall would answer, and the tape mailed back to the Pentagon. It was not long before Forrest C.Pogue, seated at Marshall's desk in his office at the Pentagon, or in the Marshall Foundation in Lexington, was well into note taking in preparation for volume one, *Education of a General*, published in 1963.

George C. Marshall wrote to Rose Page Wilson's sister, "My autobiography is an old story. . . The Foundation at the Virginia Military Institute is starting on a write-up based on the records—official and personal. I agree to fill in the blind spots. . ." and that is exactly what he did, for as long as he could. By the spring of 1957, General Marshall complained of not being able to remember details. He put off answering questions time and again and, after he returned to Leesburg from Pinehurst, he was only answering short questions with a yes or no. The interviews seemed to be finished.

**The General visits with Johnny Bertrand,
his next-door neighbor, in Pinehurst.**

Paul H. Griffith, of Uniontown, Pennsylvania presents a lifetime membership in the American Legion to General George C. Marshall.

Marshall receives the Woodrow Wilson Award, October, 1956, as Mrs. Marshall and Mrs. Woodrow Wilson watch.

Luckily, Marshall consented to having his biography written when he did, or we would not know as much as we do about his childhood and younger days. The tapes at the Marshall Library are fascinating, because of the voices and the occasional household noises. Dr. Larry I. Bland and staff have transcribed all of the tapes into a book. Nineteen tapes take up a lot of space, but now they are printed in one big book with an equally long title, *George C. Marshall Interviews and Reminiscences for Forrest C. Pogue* that can be quite helpful to someone who is researching the life of George C. Marshall. A few of Pogue's questions remained unanswered.

During his retirement years, George C. Marshall turned down numerous speaking invitations and requests to sponsor various fundraisers, but he also received many awards, honorary memberships, and he helped when he could. Some he accepted in person. Among them was a lifetime membership in the American Legion, presented to him in his hometown of Uniontown, Pennsylvania, by Colonel Paul H. Griffith. Colonel Griffith, the 1946-47 National Commander of the American Legion and a decorated veteran of both World Wars II and II, was also a native of Uniontown. In December of 1951, General Marshall introduced the national television fund-raising show for the United Cerebral Palsy Association. The Woodrow Wilson Award for Distinguished Service was presented to Marshall in October of 1956. A long list of civilian awards, memberships, and honorary degrees can be found on the Marshall Foundation web site, www.marshallfoundation.org.

In August of 1958, the General went to Walter Reed Hospital for the removal of a cyst on his eye and for some dental work. After a week or so, he was planning to go home, but he had a fall and broke a rib. Healing took awhile, but he improved at a good rate, ate well, and gained some weight. Yet, he had another problem, perhaps due to an inner ear condition, that caused him to wobble and stumble easily when walking. A sturdy cane came in handy, then. The Marshalls decided to go to Pinehurst earlier than usual that autumn.

In October 1958, Queen Frederika of Greece came to visit the Marshalls. The people of Pinehurst were impressed, and General Marshall was pleased, even though he was ill and unable to visit with her long. He was getting weaker, and spent most of his time in bed. Rose Page Wilson, was living in North Carolina also, and saw in the paper that Queen Frederika had visited the Marshalls. She had not heard from Colonel Marshall for some time, but she waited a few more weeks before calling on the Marshalls.

When Rose phoned Mrs. Marshall and inquired about her god-father, Katherine told her that he was not well, and when Rose asked what was wrong, Katherine said, "Just about everything is wrong with him…. but I think he would enjoy seeing you." Mrs. Marshall sounded very tired, Rose thought.

George C. Marshall was glad as always to see Rose. She was like a daughter to him. He had known her since she was eight years old, watched her grow, marry, and raise a family. Her oldest son, Page, was Marshall's godson, also. He enjoyed hearing about her children and her busy life. They talked at length before he said, "I have so much time now to remember." He did not talk of his career or his public life, but of his days as a boy in Pennsylvania. Rose was encouraged because he did not wander aimlessly in his memories; he was clear-headed and entertaining.

"This morning I was thinking of my father, and about the brisk, snowy winters in Uniontown. When I was very small, my father would sometimes take me tobogganing down a steep hill right in the center of town." He smiled at her. "What great sport that was!"

During the fall months, Rose visited often with the Marshalls. General Marshall talked about other things with Rose, and frequently mentioned how good Katherine was in caring for him. He was concerned that Rose should help Katherine prepare for the time when he would die. Rose found it too difficult to think about, and tried to avoid the subject. Katherine came to depend on Rose to sit with the General, and felt free to go to the store, get her hair fixed, or just take a nap. Rose knew she needed to take breaks, and was glad that she could help. She visited off and on through the Christmas holidays, but then her visits came to an end. Her Colonel Marshall took a turn for the worse. One might say he had rounded third base, and was headed for home.

* * * * *

Man Behind the Plan

Chapter 17

Saying Good-Bye

January —- October 1959

The Marshalls spent a quiet Christmas, toasted his birthday, and started the New Year in Pinehurst. The General seemed to be on the mend, somewhat. He was sometimes unsteady on his feet, and another fall would be dangerous. His doctors at Walter Reed Hospital had arranged for medical corpsmen from Fort Bragg to sit beside his door, twenty-four hours a day if necessary, whenever he was in his bedroom, just in case he needed help. He might not have known it, but it helped Mrs. Marshall rest easier, knowing help was ready if they should need it.

One night early in the New Year, the meds heard strangling sounds, rushed in, and found the General had suffered a serious stroke. He had swallowed his tongue. They saved his life by giving first aid, and took him, unconscious, by ambulance to the Army hospital at Fort Bragg. The stroke was a bad one, crippling General Marshall and leaving him weak.

Mrs. Marshall phoned Rose Page Wilson not to come to see her "Colonel Marshall" on her usual visiting day. She said that he had had a "little attack" and was at the Fort Bragg Hospital, and they would let her know when she could come again. About a month later, she received that call.

On Valentine's Day, Rose Wilson went to the hospital, knocked on the door of the VIP suite, and found the General in a good mood, and in his vibrating bed. He demonstrated the bed he called his "jiggly bed" and said it made him "feel like a hula dancer," but it was good for his circulation. She said later that General Marshall looked thinner than ever, and was somewhat confused and distracted during their conversation.

He finally told her "I want to ask you something very confidentially." He said he expected her to tell him the truth. Puzzled, she said she would answer as best she could. He finally said, "Rose, I'm not sure where I am." He did not want to ask Katherine, the orderlies, the nurses or the doctors, but he really did not know. He thought he was at Walter Reed Hospital. She told him he was in Womack Hospital at Fort Bragg. He thanked her for telling him.

Later in the day, Mrs. Marshall brought in a present for Rose. General Marshall wanted to give her something for Valentine's Day, Katherine told her. Since it was a Sunday, and an unexpected request, Mrs. Marshall brought Rose a trinket container she had at home. Rose accepted it graciously, knowing it was his thought that counted, not the gift. That was the last time that Rose Wilson saw her Colonel Marshall to talk to, but she wrote in *General Marshall Remembered*, "Some officer telephoned me in March to tell me that Colonel Marshall had . . .been moved to Walter Reed Hospital in Washington, DC."

By the spring, he made a slight comeback, and recovered enough to sit in a wheelchair and sometimes talk, if only in a whisper. His friends, both famous and non-famous, visited General Marshall. During the months he was still conscious, some of his visitors helped him relive the past. He talked with General Herron, from pre-WWI days, and with General Bull of Fort Benning days. He even talked to some by telephone.

Then, a series of brain spasms took away his sight, his hearing, and his speech. He stayed alive due to machines. President Eisenhower had his personal physician, Major General Howard Snyder, make a daily visit to Marshall's bedside. Marshall's doctor from the Fort Benning and Vancouver Barracks days, Major General Morrison Strayer, came from Carlisle, Pennsylvania to see him, but finally said, "I can't come anymore. He is paying the price of a strong constitution."

Mrs. Marshall stayed in her General's room or in a nearby cottage, coming and going through a back hospital entrance, to avoid reporters and the curious. She, too, was less physically strong than she had once been, but was with him continually during those long months.

Forrest C. Pogue was able to keep up with Marshall's condition with the help of Colonel C.J. George, who sat in the Pentagon office next to General Marshall's office where Pogue was then writing his first volume of his Marshall biography. Of course, hundreds of cards and letters arrived for him. His enemies even sent disturbing messages, relentless in their criticisms of him. If Marshall had been able to understand and read his messages, he would have welcomed the good wishes and ignored the others. Unkind and critical words never bothered him. He had done his best.

In September, Rose Wilson came to Walter Reed Hospital to see her godfather. Rose was distressed when Mrs. Marshall told her that the General was in a coma, and had not known anyone for several weeks, not even her. Mrs. Marshall told her, "I want you to know that you are specially honored to be allowed to see George. I permit very few people to see him." Presidents Truman and Eisenhower plus Sir Winston Churchill had visited. "Mr. Churchill didn't say a word; he just stood in the doorway with tears in his eyes."

George C. Marshall died at 6:08 p.m. on October 16, 1959. The date was a few months short of his 79th birthday, and one day after the 29th anniversary of his marriage to Katherine Tupper Brown. His death was not unexpected, and the plans for his funeral had started long before his last evening.

Before his stroke, Marshall had talked with his family and his aide, Colonel C.J. George, about what he wanted and what he did not want to happen at his funeral. On his way to Oslo, in 1953, he had told Colonel George, "I don't want a state funeral" and Colonel George had answered that if he did not leave specific instructions against it, one would surely happen. In 1956, he wrote out his final orders, and he expected those orders to be followed. For the most part, they were.

His service did not take place in the National Cathedral, nor did he "lie in state" in the Capital Rotunda. The military minister at the National Cathedral who had been with Marshall in China in 1924 and was the U.S. Army Chief of Chaplains in 1945, Colonel Luther Miller, was in charge of the service and the prayers. George C. Marshall did not want a lengthy eulogy.

General Marshall did not want an invitation list made up for special guests. His burial was to be private with only his family and a few friends there. He made a short list of pallbearers, and they were: Lt. Col. Clarence James George—his postwar aide, Master

**Bethlehem Chapel, National Cathedral, Washington, D.C.,
October 19, 1959.**

Sergeant William J. Heffner—- his postwar orderly, Robert A. Lovett
—- his friend and his under secretary of both state and defense,
Colonel Frank McCarthy—Secretary General Staff WWII, Master
Sergeant James W. Powder —- his chief wartime orderly, and
General Walter Bedell Smith—- an aide and staff member of several
years. He added Ambassador James Bruce to the list in case one of
the others could not be there. The rest was left to Mrs. Marshall. She
chose: Colonel William M. Spencer of Chicago, Illinois, Colonel
Robert H. Fletcher, Admiral Harold R. Stark, General Omar Bradley,
General Maxwell B. Taylor, General Charles D. Herron, Army Chief
of Staff General Lyman L. Lemnitzer, and two VMI cadets, James H.
Tumlin and Carl A. Benner.

As he had requested, George C. Marshall did not lie in state at
the Capitol, but Mrs. Marshall arranged for his unopened casket to
rest overnight in the Bethlehem Chapel at the National Cathedral
on October 19, and a large, silent crowd walked past to pay their
respects. The Army, Navy, Air Force, Marines, Coast Guard, and the
VMI corps of cadets were represented in the honor guard.

Both Benner and Tumlinson remember being pallbearers. They
were both First Classmen at VMI in October of 1959, and Tumlinson
was First Captain, as Marshall had been in 1901. They were selected
by their school officials after Marshall's first stroke and put on alert,
knowing he was seriously ill.

Jim Tumlinson said, "We considered it a great honor to participate in the funeral of General Marshall. . . We were on our way to a
football game when we heard on the radio that General Marshall
had died. We stopped the bus and I called back to the Institute for
instructions. We were told to go directly to Washington on Sunday
to the barracks where the ceremonial guards were stationed. The
teams were formed and we practiced all the ceremonies that we
would participate in. . . The ceremonies went off without a hitch. At
the conclusion of the service at the grave, the flag that covered the
casket was folded and I handed it to a representative of the family
who took it to Mrs. Marshall."

Benner said, "Yes, I was a pallbearer for General of the Army
George C. Marshall. There were two casket-bearing teams, one at
the gravesite for the burial, and one at the church (Fort Myer

Fort Myer Chapel, October 20, 1959

James H. Tumlinson,
VMI Class of 1960

Carl A. Benner,
VMI Class of 1960

Chapel) for the ceremony. . . (it was) one of the significant moments in my life."

The twenty-minute funeral service was at Ft. Myer Chapel, on a beautiful autumn day that certainly would have met with the general's approval. Mrs. Marshall and the Army Chief of Staff amended General Marshall's orders slightly by having telegrams sent to his personal staff, past and present, advising them of the time and place of the service. They included Joe Abbott, the General's long-time barber. Several of Marshall's colleagues including Ambassador Robert Murphy and Lieutenant General Lucius Clay called to ask permission to attend. Sergeant Richard Wing, the orderly who had been with Marshall during the China Mission and in Moscow, came to ask if he, too, could be seated. Colonel C.J. George asked Forrest C. Pogue, Marshall's official biographer, to sit with Sergeant Wing near the front, directly behind Mr. and Mrs. Dean Acheson.

President Dwight D. Eisenhower and his aide, Harry Vaughn, President Harry S. Truman and his aide, Robert Shultz, sat together in the same pew across the aisle from Mrs. Marshall. Her daughter, Molly, and family sat with Mrs. Marshall. Rose Page Wilson, her husband, John, and son, Page, attended the chapel service, but not the burial.

Mrs. Wilson wrote, "I heard the muffled drums sounding the approach of Colonel Marshall's flag-draped casket, and I stood up as if I were a robot. I could feel nothing—my mind was absolutely blank. The brief Episcopal service was soon over and I hadn't heard a word."

The service was short and simple, just as he had requested. Chaplain Miller's only reference to Marshall was in a prayer, "take Thy servant George," After the service, the casket was placed on a caisson and the honor guard, the family and the pallbearers moved from the chapel to the grave. There was no formal procession, no funeral dirge, or horse with empty saddle.

Mrs. Marshall walked slowly from the chapel wearing a heavy black veil and holding the arm of her son-in-law, Colonel James Winn. Molly and her son followed with her two daughters close behind, their braids tied with black ribbons.

Only the family and a few close friends went with the General to his resting place in Arlington National Cemetery, a spot in Section 7, just down the hill from the Tomb of the Unknown Soldier. From Rose Page Wilson's book, "I watched the cars disappear slowly around the curve. When they were out of sight, an almost uncontrollable panic seized me. Colonel Marshall was gone! He was gone!"

Forrest C. Pogue wrote, "In the sunlit afternoon, those remaining in the chapel, heard the sharp volleys of gunfire (the 21-gun salute) by the honor guard followed by the slow, silver sound of taps."

George C. Marshall's long and faithful tour of duty and service was finished. He was a dedicated servant of his nation and mankind. He was not perfect, his faults were human, but he was a hero in an age that needed heroes. For our day and time, his life is an echo that beckons peace and freedom, if only we can hear it. Perhaps you will be one who does.

*　*　*　*　*

Citation by President Harry S. Truman
To
General of the Army George C. Marshall
November 26, 1945

In a war unparalleled in magnitude and in horror, millions of Americans gave their country outstanding service. General of the Army George C. Marshall gave it victory.

By favor of Providence, General Marshall became Chief of Staff of the United States Army on the day that Germany attacked Poland. His was the vision that brought into being the greatest military force in history. Because he was able to make the Allies understand the true potentiality of American greatness in personnel and material, he was able to exercise greater influence than any other man on the strategy of victory.

It was he who first recognized that victory in a global war would depend on this nation's capacity to ring the earth with far-flung supply lines, to arm every willing Ally and to overcome the aggressor nations with superior fire power. He was the first to see the technological cunning and consequent greater danger of the Nazi enemy. He was the master proponent of a ground assault across the English Channel into the plains of Western Europe directed by a single Supreme Allied Commander. He insisted on maintaining unremitting pressure against the Japanese, thereby preventing them from becoming entrenched in their stolen empire and enabling our timely advances across the Pacific. He obtained from Congress the stupendous sums that made possible the atomic bomb, well knowing that failure would be his full responsibility.

Statesman and soldier, he had courage, fortitude, and vision and best of all a rare self-effacement. He has been a tower of strength as counselor of two Commanders in Chief. His standards of character, conduct and efficiency inspired the entire Army, the nation and the world. To him, as much as to any individual, the United States owes its future. He takes his place at the head of the great commanders in history

Secretary of State
George C. Marshall's Speech
Harvard University, June 5, 1947

President Dr. Conant, Members of the Board of Overseers, Ladies, and Gentlemen: I am profoundly grateful and touched by the great distinction and honor, a great compliment, accorded me by the authorities of Harvard this morning. I am overwhelmed as a matter of fact and I am rather fearful of my inability to maintain such a high rating as you have been generous enough to accord to me. In these historic and lovely surroundings, this perfect day and this very wonderful assembly, it is a tremendously impressive thing to an individual in my position. But to speak more seriously:

I need not tell you that the world situation is very serious. That must be apparent to all intelligent people. I think one difficulty is that the problem is one of such enormous complexity that the very mass of facts presented to the public by press and radio make it exceedingly difficult for the man in the street to reach a clear appraisement of the situation. Furthermore, the people of this country are distant from the troubled areas of the earth and it is hard for them to comprehend the plight and consequent reactions of the long-suffering peoples of Europe and the effect of those reactions on their governments in connections with our efforts to promote peace in the world.

In considering the requirements for the rehabilitation of Europe, the physical loss of life, the visible destruction of cities, factories, mines, and railroads was correctly estimated, but it has become obvious during recent months that this visible destruction was probably less serious than the dislocation of the entire fabric of European economy. For the past ten years, conditions have been highly abnormal. The feverish preparation for war and the more feverish maintenance of the war effort engulfed all aspects of national economies. Machinery has fallen into disrepair or is entirely under the arbitrary and destructive Nazi rule; virtually every possible enterprise was geared into the German war machine. Long-standing commercial ties, private institutions, banks, insurance companies and shipping companies disappeared, through loss of capital, absorption through nationalization or by simple destruction. In many countries, confidence in the local currency has been severely shaken. The breakdown of business structure of Europe during the war was complete. Recovery has been seriously retarded by the fact that two years after the close of hostilities a peace settlement with Germany and Austria has not been agreed upon. But even given a more prompt solution of these difficult problems, the rehabilitation of the economic structure of Europe quite evidently will require a much longer time and greater effort than had been foreseen.

There is a phase of this matter which is both interesting and serious. The farmer has always produced the foodstuffs to exchange with the city dweller for the other necessities of life. This division of labor is the basis of modern civilization. At the present time it is threatened with breakdown. The town and city industries are not producing adequate goods to exchange with the food-producing farmer. Raw materials and fuel are in short supply. Machinery, as I have said, is lacking or worn out. The farmer or peasant cannot find the goods for sale which he desires to purchase. So the sale of his farm produce for money which he cannot use seems to him and unprofitable transaction. He, therefore, has withdrawn many fields of crop cultivation and is using them for grazing. He feeds more grain to the stock and finds for himself and his family an ample supply of food, however short he may be on clothing and the other ordinary gadgets of civilization. Meanwhile people in the cities are short of food and fuel and in some places approaching starvation limits. So the governments are forced to use their foreign money and credits to procure these necessities abroad. This process exhausts funds which are urgently needed for reconstruction. Thus, a very serious situation is rapidly developing which bodes no good for the world. The modern system of the division of labor upon which the exchange of products is based is in danger of breaking down.

The truth of the matter is that Europe's requirements for the next three or four years of foreign food and other essential products—principally from America—-are so much greater that her present ability to pay that she must have substantial additional help, or face economic, social and political deterioration of a very grave character.

The remedy seems to lie in breaking the vicious circle and restoring the confidence of the people of Europe and the economic future of their own countries and of Europe as a whole. The manufacturer and the farmer throughout wide areas must be able and willing to exchange their products for currencies the continuing value of which is not open to question.

Aside from the demoralizing effect on the world at large and the possibilities of disturbances arising as a result of the desperation of the people concerned, the consequences to the economy of the United States should be apparent to all. *It is logical that the United States should do whatever it is able to do to assist in the return of normal economic health in the world, without which there can be no political stability and no assured peace. Our policy is directed not against any country or doctrine but against hunger, poverty, desperation and chaos.* Its purpose should be the revival of a working economy in the world so as to permit the emergence of political and social conditions in which free institutions can exist. Such assistance, I am convinced, must not be o a piecemeal basis as various crises develop. Any assistance that this Government may render in the future should provide a cure rather than a mere palliative. *Any government that is willing to assist in the task of recovery will find full cooperation, I am sure, on the part of the United States Government. Any government that maneuvers to block the recovery of other countries cannot expect help from us.* (Applause) Furthermore, governments, political parties, or groups that seek to perpetuate human misery in order to profit therefrom politically or otherwise will encounter the opposition off the United States. (Applause)

It is already evident that, before the United States Government can proceed much further in its efforts to alleviate the situation and help start the European world on its way to recovery there must be some agreement among the countries of Europe as to the requirement of the situation and the part those countries themselves will take in order to give proper effect to whatever action might be undertaken by this Government. It would be neither fitting nor efficacious (effective) for our Government to undertake to draw up unilaterally a program designed to place Europe on it feet economically. This it the business of the Europeans. The initiative, I think, must come from Europe. The role of this country should consist of friendly aid in the drafting of a European program and of later support of such a program so far as it is practical for us to do so. This program should be a joint one, agreed to by a number, if not all European nations.

An essential part of any successful action on the part of the United States is an understanding on the part of the people of America of the character of the problem and the remedies to be applied. Political passion and prejudice should have no part. With foresight, and a willingness on the part of our people to face up to the vast responsibilities which history has clearly placed upon our country, the difficulties I have outlined can and will be overcome. I am sorry that on each occasion I have said something publicly in regard to our international situation, I have been forced by the necessities of the case to enter into rather technical discussions. But to my mind it is of vast importance that our people reach some general understanding of what the complications really are rather than react from a passion or a prejudice or an emotion of the moment. As I said more formally a moment ago, we are remote from the scene of these troubles. It is virtually impossible at this distance merely by reading or listening or even seeing photographs and motion pictures to grasp at the real significance of the situation. Yet, the whole world's future hangs on a proper judgment, it hangs, I think, to a large extent on the realization of the American people of just what are the very dominant factors, what are the reactions of the people, what are the justifications of those reactions, what are the sufferings, what is needed, what can be done, what must be done. Thank you very much.

Timeline of The Marshall Plan

Jan. 21, 1947:   Gen. George C. Marshall becomes Secretary of State.

Jan. 25, 1947:   The first of several blizzards buries Britain and any hope of economic recovery

Feb. 21, 1947:   The British inform the United States that they can no longer support Greece and Turkey against communist expansion

March 5, 1947:   Undersecretary of State Dean Acheson asks the State-War- Navy Coordinating Committee to see which other nations need aid.

March 10, 1947:   George C. Marshall goes to Moscow for a meeting with the foreign ministers of the Britain, France, and the Soviet Union open to decide the future of Germany.

March 12, 1947:   President Harry S Truman asks Congress to aid Greece and Turkey and any other country threatened by aggression. His proposal is called "the Truman Doctrine."

April 24, 1947:   Unable to agree after 43 sessions at their Moscow meeting on Germany's future, the four foreign ministers call it quits.

April 28-29, 1947:   George C. Marshall returns from Moscow disillusioned with the Soviets and is worried about the conditions in all of Europe he says, "The patient is sinking while the doctors deliberate." He demands the State Department form a Policy Planning Staff immediately and draw up a possible plan of action for a European Recovery Plan

April-May 1947:   William Clayton, undersecretary of state, tours Europe' s devastation and tells Marshall urgent action is needed

May 6, 1947:   Dean Acheson of the State Department in a speech in Mississippi, says, Europe' s problems are also America's

May 15, 1947:   Congress approves aid to Greece and Turkey. May 23, 1947: State Department study group outlines the European Recovery Plan.

May 28, 1947:   Marshall agrees to speak at Harvard's graduation on June 5.

June 5, 1947:   In the speech that gives birth to the Marshall Plan, the Secretary of State invites Europe to petition the United States for aid.

June 6, 1947:   British Foreign Minister Ernest Bevin summons his staff to an emergency Sunday session.

June 30, 1947:   The Soviets refuse to take part in the Marshall Plan.

July 3, 1947:   British Foreign Minister Ernest Bevin and his French counterpart, Georges Bidault, invite 22 European nations to meet and consider a recovery plan.

July 12,1947:   Representatives of 16 European nations arrive in Paris to respond to Marshall's offer.

Dec. 15, 1947   Congress approves $522 million emergency aid to Europe

Dec. 19, 1947:   Truman gives the special session a Marshall Plan recommendation of $17 billion over four years. (In the end, the total was $13.6 billion.)

January 1948:   Congress opens what will become three months of debate and deliberation on the Marshall Plan.

Jan. 5, 1948:   *Time* magazine selects Marshall as "Man of the Year."

March 17, 1948:   Truman asks Congress to pass the Marshall Plan.

April 2, 1948:   Congress gives final approval to the Marshall Plan.

April 3, 1948:   Truman's signature puts the Marshall Plan into effect.

April 5, 1948:   Studebaker president Paul Hoffman, a Republican, agrees to head the agency that will carry out the Marshall Plan.

April 14, 1948:   The first shipment of Marshall Plan aid left Texas for France.

Nobel Peace Prize Lecture

George C. Marshall

December 11, 1953

I have been greatly and surprisingly honored in the past twenty-four hours, and in return, I have been requested to speak here tonight. While no subject has been suggested, it is quite evident that the cause of peace is preeminent in your minds.

Discussions without end have been devoted to the subject of peace, and the efforts to obtain a general and lasting peace have been frequent through many years of world history. There has been success temporarily, but all have broken down, and with the most tragic consequences since 1914. What I would like to do is point our attention to some directions in which efforts to attain peace seem promising of success.

I will try to phrase my views or suggestions in the simplest possible terms though I lack the magic and artistry of that great orator whom the Nobel Committee in Stockholm so appropriately honored yesterday1. In making my statement I will assume your familiarity with the discussions and efforts of the past eight years and also with something of the conditions which have governed each long continued peace in world history.

I would like to make special mention of the years of the Pax Romana, which endured through almost all of the first two centuries of the Christian era. I do so because of a personal incident which made a profound impression on me in the spring of 1919. Arriving late at night in Chaumont, the American Headquarters in France, I sought shelter for the night in the house of a group of friends. I found they were temporarily absent; so I selected an unoccupied room and looked about for a book to read as I waited for sleep to come. The books available were mostly in French or German. Since I was unable to read them with facility, I looked further and finally found an English textbook on the history of Gaul. Casting about for an interesting portion, I landed on a description of the famous Roman Peace. Included in this description was a statement of the dispositions of the Roman troops during this prolonged period, a legion at Cologne, another at Coblenz, a third at Mayence, and the reserve at Trier. Now those happened to be the identical dispositions of our Allied Forces some eighteen hundred years later, with the Peace Commission sitting in Paris and evolving the policy of the League of Nations.

I would not wish to imply that the military deployment I have just described corresponds to the protective NATO deployment of today. The threat today is quite different, but I do think that this remarkable historical repetition does suggest that we have walked blindly, ignoring the lessons of the past, with, in our century, the tragic consequences of two world wars and the Korean struggle as a result.

In my country, my military associates frequently tell me that we Americans have learned our lesson. I completely disagree with this contention and point to the rapid disintegration between 1945 and 1950 of our once vast power for maintaining the peace. As a direct consequence, in my opinion, there resulted the brutal invasion of South Korea, which for a time threatened the complete defeat of our hastily arranged forces in that field. I speak of this with deep feeling because in 1939 and again in the early fall of 1950 it suddenly became my duty, my responsibility, to rebuild our national military strength in the very face of the gravest emergencies.

These opening remarks may lead you to assume that my suggestions for the advancement of world peace will rest largely on military strength. For the moment the maintenance of peace in the present hazardous world situation does depend in very large measure on military power, together with Allied cohesion. But the maintenance of large armies for an indefinite period is not a practical or a promising basis for policy. We must stand together strongly for these present years, that is, in this present situation; but we must, I repeat, we must find another solution, and that is what I wish to discuss this evening.

There has been considerable comment over the awarding of the Nobel Peace Prize to a soldier. I am afraid this does not seem as remarkable to me as it quite evidently appears to others. I know a great deal of the horrors and tragedies of war. Today, as chairman of the American Battle Monuments Commission, it is my duty to supervise the construction and maintenance of military cemeteries in many countries overseas, particularly in Western Europe. The cost of war in human lives is constantly spread before me, written neatly in many ledgers whose columns are gravestones. I am deeply moved to find some means or method of avoiding another calamity of war. Almost daily I hear from the wives, or mothers, or families of the fallen. The tragedy of the aftermath is almost constantly before me.

I share with you an active concern for some practical method for avoiding war. Let me first say that I regard the present highly dangerous situation as a very special one, which naturally dominates our thinking on the subject of peace, but which should not, in my opinion, be made the principal basis for our reasoning towards the manner for securing a condition of long continued peace. A very strong military posture is vitally necessary today. How long it must continue I am not prepared to estimate, but I am sure that it is too narrow a basis on which to build a dependable, long-enduring peace. The guarantee for a long continued peace will depend on other factors in addition to a moderated military strength, and no less important. Perhaps the most important single factor will be a spiritual regeneration to develop goodwill, faith, and understanding among nations. Economic factors will undoubtedly play an important part. Agreements to secure a balance of power, however disagreeable they may seem, must likewise be considered. And with all these there must be wisdom and the will to act on that wisdom.

In this brief discussion, I can give only a very limited treatment of these great essentials to peace. However, I would like to select three more specific areas for closer attention.

The first relates to the possibilities of better education in the various factors affecting the life of peaceful security, both in terms of its development and of its disruption. Because wisdom in action in our Western democracies rests squarely upon public understanding, I have long believed that our schools have a key role to play. Peace could, I believe, be advanced through careful study of all the factors, which have gone into the various incidents now historical that have marked the breakdown of peace in the past. As an initial procedure our schools, at least our colleges but preferably our senior high schools, as we call them, should have courses which not merely instruct our budding citizens in the historical sequence of events of the past, but which treat with almost scientific accuracy the circumstances which have marked the breakdown of peace and have led to the disruption of life and the horrors of war.

There may perhaps have been a "last clear chance" to avoid the tragic conflagrations of our century. In the case of World War II, for example, the challenge may well have come in the early thirties, and passed largely unrecognized until the situation was unlikely to be retrieved. We are familiar with specific events such as the march into the Rhineland or aggression in Ethiopia or Manchuria. Perhaps there was also a last clear chance to begin to build up the strength of the democracies to keep the military situation in equilibrium. There may also have been a last clear chance to penetrate to the spirit of the peoples of the nations threatening the peace, and to find ways of peaceful adjustment in the economic field as well. Certainly, had the outcome of the war, with its devastation and disruption, been foreseen, and had there been an understanding on all sides of the problems that were threatening the peace, I feel sure that many possibilities for accommodation would have been much more thoroughly explored.

It is for this reason that I believe our students must first seek to understand the conditions, as far as possible without national prejudices, which have led to past tragedies and should strive to determine the great fundamentals which must govern a peaceful progression toward a constantly higher level of civilization. There are innumerable instructive lessons out of the past, but all too frequently their presentation is highly colored or distorted in the effort to present a favorable national point of view. In our school histories at home, certainly in years past, those written in the North present a strikingly different picture of our Civil War from those written in the South. In some portions, it is hard to realize they are dealing with the same war. Such reactions are all too common in matters of peace and security. But we are told that we live in a highly scientific age. Now the progress of science depends on facts and not fancies or prejudice. Maybe in this age we can find a way of facing the facts and discounting the distorted records of the past.

I am certain that a solution of the general problem of peace must rest on broad and basic understanding on the part of its peoples. Great single endeavors like a League of Nations, a United Nations, and undertakings of that character, are of great importance and in fact, absolutely necessary, but they must be treated as steps toward the desired end.

We must depend in large measure on the impartiality of those who teach. Their approach must be on a scientific basis in order to present the true facts. The scientists, no matter of what nationality, make a common approach to their problems.

For my second suggestion, I would like to consider the national attitudes that bear on the great problem of peace. I hope you will not think me amiss if I turn to my own country and certain rather special circumstances found there to illustrate my point. Despite the amazing conquest of the air and its reduction of distances to a matter of hours and not days, or minutes instead of hours, the United States is remote in a general sense from the present turbulent areas of the world. I believe the measure of detachment, limited though it is, has been of help in enabling us on occasion to take an impartial stand on heated international problems.

Also, my country is very specially constituted in terms of population. We have many families of Norwegian ancestry in our population. My country also includes large numbers of former citizens of many of the other countries of Europe, including the present satellite states. I recall that when the first Polar flight was made by the Russians from Moscow over the top of the world to land on the little airfield of the post I commanded at Vancouver on the Columbia River in the state of Washington, my home was surrounded within a few hours by hundreds and hundreds of Russians, all presumably citizens of the United States. Italians, Turks, Greeks, and many, many others who came to our country now constitute an organic portion of our population.

From this fact, we have acquired, I think, a feeling and a concern for the problems of other peoples. There is a deep urge to help the oppressed and to give aid to those upon whom great and sudden hardship has fallen.

We, naturally, cannot see a problem in the exact terms as people like yourselves or the Danes, or the Dutch, or the French, for example - people living in the closest contact with each other, yet widely differing in national heritage. I believe there is, however, a readiness to cooperate which is one of the great and hopeful factors of the world of today. While we are not in close contact with the details of problems, neither are we indifferent to them, and we are not involved in your historical tensions and suspicions.

If I am correct in thinking that these factors have given us as a nation some advantage in the quest for peace, then I would suggest that principles of cooperation based on these factors might contribute to a better understanding amongst all nations.

I realize fully that there is another side to this picture. In America, we have not suffered the destruction of our homes, our towns, and our cities. We have not been enslaved for long periods, at the complete mercy of a conqueror. We have enjoyed freedom in its fullest sense. In fact, we have come to think in terms of freedom and the dignity of the individual more or less as a matter of course, and our apparent unconcern until times of acute crisis presents a difficult problem to the citizens of the countries of Western Europe, who have seldom been free from foreign threat to their freedom, their dignity, and their security. I think nevertheless that the people of the United States have fully demonstrated their willingness to fight and die in the terrible struggle for the freedom we all prize, to sacrifice their own men in large numbers for this common cause, and to contribute vast sums for the general benefit of the Western countries.

I recognize that there are bound to be misunderstandings under the conditions of wide separation between your countries and mine. However, I believe the attitude of cooperation has been thoroughly proven. I also believe that the participation of millions of our young men and women in the struggle in Western Europe, in the closest contact with your people, will bring as its result less of misunderstanding on our side of the Atlantic than perhaps on yours.

In my own case, for example, I spent two and one half years in France during the First World War. Frequently I was quartered in the households of the French peasantry and spent long evenings by the kitchen fires, talking far into the night. I came to know them well, admired them, and in some cases came to love them. Now, how many do you suppose of the present citizens of Western

Europe have had a similar look-in on the homes of people in the farms and small towns of America. A few may know much of New York, Washington, and Chicago, but those great cities do not represent the heart of America.

The third area I would like to discuss has to do with the problem of the millions who live under subnormal conditions and who have now come to a realization that they may aspire to a fair share of the God-given rights of human beings. Their aspirations present a challenge to the more favored nations to lend assistance in bettering the lot of the poorer. This is a special problem in the present crisis, but it is of basic importance to any successful effort toward an enduring peace. The question is not merely one of self-interest arising from the fact that these people present a situation, which is a seedbed for either one or the other of two greatly differing ways of life. Ours is democracy, according to our interpretation of the meaning of that word. If we act with wisdom and magnanimity, we can guide these yearnings of the poor to a richer and better life through democracy.

We must present democracy as a force holding within itself the seeds of unlimited progress by the human race. By our actions, we should make it clear that such a democracy is a means to a better way of life, together with a better understanding among nations. Tyranny inevitably must retire before the tremendous moral strength of the gospel of freedom and self-respect for the individual, but we have to recognize that these democratic principles do not flourish on empty stomachs, and that people turn to false promises of dictators because they are hopeless and anything promises something better than the miserable existence that they endure. However, material assistance alone is not sufficient. The most important thing for the world today in my opinion is a spiritual regeneration, which would reestablish a feeling of good faith among men generally. Discouraged people are in sore need of the inspiration of great principles. Such leadership can be the rallying point against intolerance, against distrust, against that fatal insecurity that leads to war. It is to be hoped that the democratic nations can provide the necessary leadership.

The points I have just discussed are, of course, no more than a very few suggestions in behalf of the cause of peace. I realize that they hold nothing of glittering or early promise, but there can be no substitute for effort in many fields. There must be effort of the spirit

- to be magnanimous, to act in friendship, to strive to help rather than to hinder. There must be effort of analysis to seek out the causes of war and the factors, which favor peace, and to study their application to the difficult problems which will beset our international intercourse. There must be material effort - to initiate and sustain those great undertakings, whether military or economic, on which world equilibrium will depend.

If we proceed in this manner, there should develop a dynamic philosophy which knows no restrictions of time or space. In America, we have a creed, which comes to us from the deep roots of the past. It springs from the convictions of the men and women of many lands who founded the nation and made it great. We share that creed with many of the nations of the Old World and the New with whom we are joined in the cause of peace. We are young in world history, but these ideals of ours we can offer to the world with the certainty that they have the power to inspire and to impel action.

I am not implying in any way that we would attempt to persuade other people to adopt our particular form of government. I refer here specifically to those fundamental values on which our government, like many other democracies, is based. These, I believe, are timeless and have a validity for all mankind. These, I believe, will kindle the imagination and arouse the spirit.

A great proponent of much of what I have just been saying is Dr. Albert Schweitzer, the world humanitarian, who today receives the Nobel Peace Award for 1952. I feel it is a vast compliment to be associated with him in these awards this year. His life has been utterly different from mine, and we should all be happy that his example among the poor and benighted of the earth should have been recognized by the Peace Award of the Nobel Committee.

I must not further complicate this discussion with the wide variety of specific considerations which will enfold the gradual growth of a sound approach toward some method of securing an enduring peace in the world. I fear, in fact I am rather certain, that due to my inability to express myself with the power and penetration of the great Churchill, I have not made clear the points that assume such prominence and importance in my mind. However, I have done my best, and I hope I have sown some seeds which may bring forth good fruit.

About the George C. Marshall Foundation

The mission of the George C. Marshall Foundation is to promote the values of selfless service, dedicated effort and strength of character exemplified by Marshall's life and leadership in war and peace, and to inspire new generations to follow his example as they face the challenges of the future.

The George C. Marshall Foundation was established in 1953 at the urging of President Harry S. Truman, who believed that succeeding generations should not be permitted to forget the career and legacy of one of our nation's greatest soldier/statesmen. Despite numerous lucrative offers, Gen. Marshall refused to write his memoirs and President Truman feared that Marshall's many accomplishments would be lost over the passage of time.

The first director of the Foundation was Forrest Pogue, a distinguished military historian and the father of oral history. Dr. Pogue conducted a series of taped interviews with Gen. Marshall, which became the primary source for Pogue's definitive four-volume biography of Gen. Marshall.

More than a million visitors have come to the library and museum, located on the post of the Virginia Military Institute, Marshall's alma mater, in Lexington, Virginia since it was dedicated in 1964. Over the years, the Marshall Foundation's library, archives and museum have expanded to become one of the world's top collections of documents, films, photographs, maps, posters and artifacts relating to "the Marshall era," loosely defined as the first half of the 20th Century.

In addition to the library, archives, and museum, the Marshall Foundation sponsors education and outreach programs for students from middle school to post graduate work. The Foundation also conducts international conferences and symposia on a variety of topics.

Since 1978, the Marshall Foundation has hosted the Marshall ROTC Award Seminar, which brings the top Army ROTC cadet from every unit in the country to Lexington for a three-day seminar on defense and national security issues. Past keynote speakers for the seminar have included President George W. Bush, Vice President Dick Cheney, and Secretary of State Colin L. Powell.

Since 1997, the Marshall Foundation has presented the Marshall Award to outstanding citizens of the world who exemplify Gen. Marshall's commitment to peace and economic development. Past recipients of the award include Helmut Kohl, David Rockefeller, George H.W. Bush, and Colin Powell.

You are cordially invited to visit the Marshall Foundation in Lexington, Virginia or to visit our website at www.marshallfounda-tion.org

Brian Shaw
Vice President of the George C. Marshall Foundation
Editor of *Topics*

BIBLIOGRAPHY

Abrams, Irwin. *The Nobel Peace Prize and the Laureates*. G.K. Hall & Co. Boston. 1988.

Bland, Larry I., Editor. *George C. Marshall Interviews and Reminiscences for Forrest C. Pogue. 3rd Edition.* Lexington, Virginia. 1996.

Cray, Ed. *General of the Army George C. Marshall, Soldier and Statesman.* Cooper Square Press. New York, NY. 1990.

George C. Marshall Foundation. [Bland, Larry I.] *"Fully Equal of the Best"; George C. Marshall and the Virginia Military Institute.* George C. Marshall Foundation. Lexington, Virginia. 1996.

Goodpaster, Andrew J. *"George C. Marshall's World, and Ours."* An editorial. New York Times. New York, NY. December 11, 2003.

Lubetkin, Wendy. *Marshall* Chelsea House Publishers, New York. 1989.

McCullough, David. *Truman*. Simon and Schuster. New York.1992.

Marshall, Katherine Tupper. *Together, Annals of an Army Wife*. Tupper and Love, Inc. New York, Atlanta. 1946.

Pogue, Forrest C. *George C. Marshall, Statesman,1945-1959* .Viking Penguin, Inc. New York. 1987.

Skutt, Mary Sutton and Thompson, Rachel Yarnell. *America's Hero to the World, George C. Marshall*. The George C. Marshall International Center and the Federal Republic of Germany. Lexington, Virginia. 1999.

Smith, Walter Bedell. *My Three Years in Moscow*. J.B. Lippincott Company. New York and Phildelphia. 1950.

Stoler, Mark A. *George C. Marshall; Soldier-Statesman of the American Century*. Twayne Publishers. New York. 1989.

Wilson, Rose Page. *General Marshall Remembered*, Prentice-Hall,Inc. Englewood Cliffs, NJ. 1968.

Woods, Randall B. *The Marshall Plan, A Fifty Year Perspective*. German Marshall Fund of the United States. Washington, D.C. 1987. Reprinted by the George C. Marshall Foundation. Lexington, Virginia. 1997.

Acknowledgements

When I finally hold the finished book, I will definitely feel a sense of gratitude, as well as one of relief and freedom. I owe many people thank yous, because I could never write a book entirely by myself. First, I thank my husband, Dick Skutt, for his constant interest and support in my subject and my writing, his patience through the publishing process, and for putting up with my gripes, and wild rantings. I thank all of my family and my friends for their patience and tolerance of forgotten birthdays, anniversaries, promises, and meetings.

I must certainly thank everyone who kept me working these past three years by so often asking, "How's the *new* book coming?", "How much longer *can* it take?", or "Aren't you done with Marshall *yet?*" among other things, all meaning about the same. I probably would not have finished without that helpful encouragement and aggravation.

I thank Jeanne Pedersen of the Marshall Foundation for her talented touch of gathering photos and creating a third beautiful book cover. Thanks to Joanne Hartog, of the Marshall Research Library, for her assistance in my sporadic search for photos. Thanks to the staff at the News-Gazette Print Shop, specifically to Jim Dedrick and Cheryl Garrett, for their guidance, kindness, and consistent good humor. Cheryl is patient beyond measure.

Of course, I thank my manuscript readers, who caught errors and asked for clarity from confusion. First, to the George C. Marshall expert, Larry I. Bland, who, for the third time, caught the slightest slip of name, date, place, or fact I offer a special thank you. Thanks to Peggy Hays, for her experienced teacher's insight and suggested improvements. Thanks, Hart Slater, for many helpful tidbits, detail censorship, and your kind and encouraging words. Thanks to Margaret and Joe Skovira for proofing the final copy on such short notice and catching those few crucial spelling errors. Thanks to granddaughters Donna Puglisi and Michelle LaFalce for their student input, and, of course, to Dick Skutt for his precise comments.Every one of you found different yet similar things, which was good. I considered all of your comments, corrections, and suggestions and I even used most of them. I do appreciate your keen eyes!

Thanks to Harry Warner for his combined opinions, ideas, and for writing an introduction. I thank Brian Shaw for his contribution concerning the Marshall Foundation history. Finally, thanks to my faithful Dublin High School friends, Nils N. Haag and Margaret L. Welsh for their long-distance assistance and interest. I truly needed and valued everyone's help.

Ten years ago I chose to take on the task of translating the George C. Marshall story from longer and thicker books into ones, sized and worded, specifically for young people. My chosen mission is now complete.

Mary Skutt
November, 2004

a very few words about the author...

Mary Sutton Skutt was born and grew up in Pulaski County, Virginia, about a hundred miles south of Lexington, shortly before George C. Marshall became a general. Her elementary and high school life happened during the years of the Marshall Plan, and her college years in Radford, Virginia paralleled Marshall's retirement years. Her first child was a year old when Marshall died in 1959, and she saw the dedication of the Marshall Foundation on the local television news in 1964, a few months before her fourth child turned one year old.

Her interest in George C. Marshall came along and grew, just as her grandchildren did, during her Lexington teaching and retirement years. She was lucky enough to be in the right place at the right time, and is happy she could write about Marshall's remarkable life for her grandchildren, and for you.